NOBLE AUTOMATION NOW

Innovate, Motivate, And Transform
With Intelligent Automation And Beyond

Christopher W. Hodges

INDIE BOOKS
INTERNATIONAL

ISBN-13: 978-1-952233-84-5
Library of Congress Control Number: 2021923342

Designed by Darren Wheeling | blackegg.com

INDIE BOOKS INTERNATIONAL®, INC.
2424 VISTA WAY, SUITE 316
OCEANSIDE, CA 92054
www.indiebooksintl.com

CONTENTS

FOREWORD

Why should I read this book? This is a question every busy executive has to ask before investing time in reading anything. Throughout my career, I have been curious and open to change but haven't had time to waste. I've rarely had the time I wanted to be completely certain in every decision but decide and act I have for better or for worse.

This book, *Noble Automation Now*, is timely given the disruptions the world is going through, which is why I think you should read it. Chris Hodges has clearly captured what it takes to imagine, envision, build, and support the game-changing possibilities of Intelligent Automation. More importantly he is encouraging all of us to take automation, robotics, and artificial intelligence to the next natural level by fully engaging our teams and serving all our constituencies thereby making it noble.

Noble Automation, as Chris has named it, raises our chances for success while preserving our valuable time, money, and focus. At Nestlé, we have made exciting progress with technology. We have improved our processes, innovated our offerings, and increased team engagement. These technologies are helping us transform our business. Technology is a game changer when leveraged smartly.

At the extremes, we can refuse to embrace the full potential of automation in a vain attempt to preserve the comfortable while jeopardizing our future. Alternatively, we could recklessly plunge fully into artificial intelligence and its accompanying hype wave hoping for a business miracle.

Neither of these appeal to me as a leader. Instead, I want our company to adopt technologies that will help us succeed and stay true to our values. To be truly successful, we must serve all our stakeholders and create shared value to the greatest degree possible, never forgetting that to do so we must first compete successfully in the global business world.

These technologies are powerful tools to serve our stakeholders, but they are ineffective if we don't lead our teams, free their creativity, and ignite their spirit toward ever more rewarding work and lives. People and technology should not just coexist, they should thrive together. *Noble Automation Now* is a call to action and adventure for leaders eager to continue to succeed, serve, and prosper into the future.

All the best!

Laurent Friexe
CEO Zone Americas Nestlé

PREFACE

We're at the beginning of an exciting journey, maybe even a hero's journey. You may be comfortable with your career and find the idea of a new journey unwelcome or even irritating, but the phone is ringing, and it won't stop until you pick it up. On the line may be your next leadership call to adventure.

If you answer, the voice will tell you the age of Intelligent Automation has arrived, bringing excitement, risk, and opportunity. Intelligent Automation combines software and hardware that allow machines to do what was once only possible with people. Examples range from simple software robots that scan emails and extract information into other systems to the truly amazing where physical robots track and move inventory, adjust shelf location, suggest sales, and maximize revenue, all in support of humans.

You may want to block the call, but this is analogous to hoping you can succeed without automation. Alternatively, answering the call means embracing the most exciting and powerful business change since the PC. What will you do?

If you dare, you could distinguish yourself further and benefit many by embracing a holistic approach and using Intelligent Automation to best serve all your stakeholders. This is Noble Automation.

This book coins the term Noble Automation as combining Intelligent Automation technology with the inspired and insightful leadership necessary to help humans be heroes. Doing so will stimulate a wave of human innovation and tap into the incredible potential of people working toward inspiring goals. Companies profit, and people thrive.

Hopefully, when you finish reading, your answer is clear, and your actions include planning your next journey. We may not have met, but I know your success and fulfillment will be contagious. If together we continue to find and deliver the value customers want, the people we care most about will have better lives. This book, my public talks, and consulting are all aimed at helping inspirational leaders succeed. I join you in your support of capitalism, the nobility of work, and the value of people.

While no two people walk the same road, you see quite a bit with enough time on any path. I've worked in twenty-four countries and lived in five. I've been a United States Naval Officer, corporate executive, consulting partner, entrepreneur, author, speaker, and coach. I have achieved successes and made huge mistakes with more people in more places than I can remember.

Whatever I have learned was from gracious men and women like you, generous enough to take the time to teach. Also, like you, I have learned both from good leadership examples and bad, from both earnest coaching and outright neglect. I hope to return the positive favor by sharing lessons on implementing automation and business transformations.

As Intelligent Automation leader for Northwest Europe at Accenture and Deloitte, I stood and sometimes nearly bled in a crucible, combining people, process, and technology. Brilliant technologists, dedicated HR leaders, and often desperate workforces were sometimes overwhelmed and paralyzed by fear and indecision, which blocked opportunity. Better decisions need to be made.

This is an epic crossroads for business and industry. Do we embrace automation or avoid it? Like the Industrial Revolution, mass production, or the creation of the computer, this crossroads is disruptive and defined by the rise of intelligent machines. Unlike the previous iterations, Intelligent Automation is happening at frantic speed. PCs didn't change the world for years after their invention. Intelligent Automation is moving in months.

Crossroads lead to different outcomes, some good and some bad. Today, we can only imagine life without mass production, yet the change was unpleasant and undesirable for many. In the 1800s, textile workers destroyed new automated looms out of fear of job loss. Yet, automation and progress won; we are all the better for it if wealth, health, longevity, and freedom are the metrics. Crossroads are indeed scary and exciting.

*"Two roads diverged in a wood, and I took the one
less traveled by, and that has made all the difference."*
Robert Frost

The two paths in this case are optimism and pessimism regarding Intelligent Automation. The optimistic path is taken from a sense of life that sees potential, growth, challenge, and fulfillment. The pessimistic path is taken from a sense of life that sees loss, fear, drudgery, and survival. The road less traveled is bold innovation like Intelligent Automation. It is optimism while embracing the new and surrendering the old.

This book is an encouraging look at Intelligent Automation today, including the tools, techniques, and implications. It includes a close look at how leaders can continue to succeed by doing this well and make their initiative Noble Automation.

This book is not a comprehensive technology map, general leadership course, or policy handbook for governments or labor unions. Automation, like waves at the beach, is unstoppable. We must all adapt.

I hope this book propels you further down the (Noble Automation) road less traveled, where we can meet to share great stories, healthy exhaustion, bold laughter, and the fulfillment that makes us happier people.

Chris

Christopher W. Hodges
Denver, Colorado
2021

PART ONE

Why Noble Automation Can Be a Life-or-Death Challenge

"Shut down all garbage mashers on the Detention Level."
Luke Skywalker to C-3PO in *Star Wars Episode IV: A New Hope*

The *Star Wars* series is about good overcoming evil and humans transcending their limitations. Humans become heroes by learning, overcoming barriers, and facing their fears. The machines help people, not replace them. In my words, it is about Noble Automation.

In the first film in 1977, our heroes confront great evil while trying to escape from within the huge Death Star spaceship. After bluffing, running, and shooting their way through overwhelming odds, they find themselves in a huge trash compactor with the walls closing in.

Luke Skywalker, the emerging rebel leader, cannot blast his way out of impending doom and death. The princess, with all her royalty and bluster, is also helpless. Even the brawn of a seven-foot-tall Wookie is impotent. Only with help from Luke's robot accomplices is disaster averted. The robots answer Luke's call, search a vast database, identify the right compactor, and free the humans just in time.

Luke, Leia, and company return to the fight, where their human traits of intelligence, courage, and empathy prevail. At critical junctions, the robots are there to do the essential supporting machine tasks. In the end, humans and robots share the stage and accolades.

In the film series, humans and noble robots save the galaxy. This book suggests we can personally save ourselves and our colleagues from unnecessary drudgery and frustration. We can be heroes.

Back On Earth

Copenhagen, Denmark is often ranked among the world's happiest places. Scandinavian business leaders are heralded for their commitment to employee well-being, gender equality, diversity, etc. Yet, the following happened while I worked there.

The CFO of a leading Nordic finance firm, seeking to improve performance and cut costs, had identified automation as an opportunity. He summoned his team to hear the plan.

He was a seasoned, smart, and successful leader who'd achieved improvements in several companies. This respected, analytical leader and likely CEO candidate backed his decisions with data.

Dutifully, his department of over one hundred people assembled and awaited their boss's announcements.

The CFO confidently walked in, prepared, focused, and Scandinavian thin. With supporting data in hand, he stood before the microphone:

Thank you for coming today, though I admit the meeting was mandatory. Before reviewing the presentation and numbers, I want to say that automation is exciting, and it is going to dramatically change the world and improve our business. In fact, half of you won't work here in two years.

Yes, he said that and reinforced the message in a press interview days later.

Questions:
- How do you think this was received?
- How would you rate the CFO's chances of success?
- As a team member, what would you have been thinking?

This real-life example is how Intelligent Automation and other technology-driven transformations can be poorly implemented. A recent McKinsey Study indicated more than 70 percent of major business transformations fail to achieve their goals.[1] The arrival of Intelligent Automation (IA) only compounds the problem.

The rate of change driven by technology is accelerating. New, more disruptive capabilities are arriving faster than ever. Paradoxically, since most changes fail, this means more value will be destroyed faster unless something changes.

Fortunately, some companies will succeed spectacularly. Will it be different this time? The data says yes, it will be both better and worse.

To be clear, you and your business may succeed with Intelligent Automation and artificial intelligence (AI) doing whatever you are doing right now. However, if your approach is shaky, you also risk destroying your competitiveness and maybe your career.

The race to stay competitive is now a multi-heat sprint where fewer competitors move forward after each run. In real running, short-distance races are often lost by minor mistakes, while long-distance runners have more time to recover. As a former hurdler, I never won a race when I stumbled early on. However, my long-distance running friends occasionally did recover from behind. The sobering reality is the life expectancy of the average CEO and senior executive is a hurdle race, not a marathon.[2]

In earlier eras, companies had many competitors and loyal customers who were less likely to switch providers. Companies could lag in some areas and then catch up over time. Switching inertia, lack of information, and deep client relationships reduced customer churn. While this is still true for some companies, most face added pressure as new technologically smarter and nimble disrupters grow.

The list of disrupted companies and industries is long. (See chart below.)

Legacy Business	Disrupters
Retail Stores	Amazon
Hotels / Vacation Rentals	Airbnb
Financial Advisers	Robo Advisers
Job Recruiters / Headhunters	LinkedIn / Indeed
Taxis / Limousines	Uber
Bespoke Manufacturing	3D Printers
Cashiers and Clerks	Self Checkout
Colleges / Preschools / Tutoring	Khan Academy
Wire Service Providers	Transfer Wise and Venmo
Your Company	*An Intelligent Automation-Enabled Startup*

Today, information flows too fast to recover from significant missteps. Consider how quickly bad customer ratings, missed deliveries, or overcharged fees can race worldwide to thousands of new or existing customers.

At one end of disruption are high-frequency stock traders who move their trading computers closer to the trading floor to save milliseconds from processing their buy/sell decisions or cloud-based, work-from-home startups that require minimal infrastructure.

At the other end of the spectrum are high-touch, relationship or experience-based businesses like theme parks and restaurants. Disney is unlikely to lose park customers through a tedious customer support line. Similarly, Michelin-starred restaurants are unlikely to lose diners because they processed their accounts payable late. If you are Mickey Mouse or the owner of a Michelin-starred restaurant, you may be safe, for now. Most companies are in the middle, and like the proverbial frog, perhaps oblivious to the rising heat.

Three Overall Implications:

1. To compete, companies must outperform with better quality, value, and speed.
2. What was enough yesterday may not be enough tomorrow.
3. There's no time for excessive debating, office politics, or fear-based paralysis.

You may say: "What else is new? We've been dealing with technology since the PC and internet." The answer is the potent and highly disruptive combination of Intelligent Automation tools and the speed of global information flows.

What Is Intelligent Automation And What Can Make It Noble?

Definition:
Intelligent Automation combines tools that interpret written, visual, and auditory data, speed up processes, execute rules, and apply increasingly complicated reasoning to solve business problems with little ongoing

human involvement. These tools are often used to bridge or supplement existing systems. We can make Intelligent Automation Noble Automation by implementing it and sharing the benefits we create with all stakeholders.

How Technology Is Typically Used Today With Little Automation:

- Computers and spreadsheets have revolutionized how we handle calculations. The spreadsheets do what humans could do but faster and without errors.

- Through email, we communicate and send information around the world. However, at the beginning and the end of nearly every email is a person and a delay.

- Enterprise resource planning (ERP) systems like Oracle and SAP are the brains of major companies, but they hold the critical information like a nearly inaccessible safe.

- Salesforce and Workday are examples of popular specialty tools companies use to manage sales and HR.

- Humans sit in the middle of these systems, like glamorless airport flight controllers, processing, moving, copying, and entering information and changes (sometimes called swivel chair computing).

- Swivel chair computing is in the bullseye of Intelligent Automation because most systems have not been integrated. System integration projects are a viable solution, but they take years to complete and often destroy profit. So, humans remain the link between various systems.

- Outsourcing companies evolved to save onshore humans from this tedious work. Offshore employees then got the joy of swivel chair computing.

- Some humans are good at this repetitive work, but those who are, are often so consumed in detail that they have little attention available for innovating or seeing new opportunities.

How This Looks With Noble Automation:

Natascha, a knowledge worker, arrives at work and opens her business dashboard.

She sees a list of exceptions, creative pursuits, and daily routines. While she focuses on important tasks, a series of automated human enablers help her work.

Examples of how automation helps:

- One robot combs the ERP for client account activity and looks for triggers that need human involvement. Another robot applies machine learning to the pattern of transactions.

- A simple report appears on Natascha's screen, suggesting a call for a specific sales opportunity. When the customer is called, he/she experiences personal attention and has an improved opinion of the company. This improved service is possible because a robot analyzed big data and allowed Natascha to be human.

- The phone rings and a client has a billing concern. A robot recognizes the incoming number and prepares a list of the most likely reasons for the call.

- Before Natascha, the agent, has said "hello," she sees the top potential reasons for the call and the information needed to quickly answer the questions.

- Later in the day, a robot handles seventeen of twenty emails waiting for Natascha with machine-learning-enabled responses and flags. The remaining three messages are queued for human intervention. Natascha handles each while relaxed and unhurried, and with professionalism.

By 10 a.m., Natascha is focused on brainstorming new revenue-generating services with her colleagues, combining their insights.

At 3 p.m., Natascha's natural energy level is rising as she completes a thirty-minute training course on communication skills. Meanwhile, the robots work on.

- As the day ends, Natascha shuts off her PC. Before she leaves, she receives a call from an internal robot with an urgent client call. Natascha confirms she can answer a client's question. The robot generates a verbal question, and she responds on her phone.

- The robot confirms Natascha's answer and emails the client within the agreed service window. The robot records the reply, and machine learning begins to build another standard reply to similar questions.

The above example may not fit your industry, but the overall trend and potential for automation and artificial intelligence to change your business is real, and so is the downside risk of job loss.

Unfortunately, media today makes its money pushing clicks and generating hype. Truth is the casualty. Press reporting on the impact of automation is no different.

Earlier Era Press:

"Will machines devour man?[3]
New York Times, 1921

"We are being afflicted with a new disease,
technological unemployment."[4]
John Maynard Keynes, 1930s

"Who will have the last laugh in the gadget age—man or machine?
Well, the machine is already giving a preliminary oily chuckle.
For it is gaining…gaining…gaining on mankind."[5]
Pulitzer Prize-winning AP writer Hal Boyle, 1949

7

Modern Era Press:

"Robots Will Replace 20 Million Jobs by 2030, Oxford Report Finds."[6]
Oxford University

"Automation could kill 73 million U.S. jobs by 2030."[7]
McKinsey & Co.

"There certainly will be job disruption. Because what's going to happen is robots will be able to do everything better than us... All of us."[8]
Elon Musk

Which is it? History and informed insiders show that the job loss will range from severe (47 percent)[9] to modest (9 percent), depending on job functions. The opportunity to "do something" depends on the industry, role, company, and most importantly, the individual.

Who Should Do Something About This?

Some leaders may say: "It's a free world. People need to take care of themselves and get marketable skills."

Opposite this, a leader may say: "It is the responsibility of government and the companies to take care of their people."

Both extremes are fallacies. This is not a policy book; it is an outline for leaders and employees to increase their probabilities of surviving and thriving in this technology revolution.

Noble Automation Now asserts that robots and Intelligent Automation can be applied for noble ends. Specifically, they can be used to bring out the best of us humans by removing drudgery, providing insights, and allowing us the time and energy to feel, think, empathize, connect, and solve problems—be human.

In the words of Laurent Freixe, EVP and CEO Zone Americas of Nestlé:

> "*When it comes to automation there are many repetitive low value-added jobs that will be lost, but at the same time we are growing and need those people to do higher value jobs. Robots make this possible...Our customers want a personalized experience and robots are the only way to do this at scale.*"[10]

Automation is essential and will march forward. Therefore, handling it well is important for companies, leaders, and employees. Leading through implementing Noble Automation and business transformations is likely to be life or death, at least at work.

Here are a few examples:

What To Avoid (Case Example #1)

Even during the peak of Jack Welch's GE success, not everything went well. One such project was named after a predatory cat and was meant to integrate multiple software platforms into a single unified operating system that would drive one of GE's core businesses.

Over eighteen months, a grotesquely bloated project scope lacking a clear owner or fixed goal became an albatross around a local business leader's neck. Project meetings with over twenty people sapped team energy and included endless arcane questions that wasted most attendees' time.

Personal incentives and project success goals were misaligned. Young, expensive consultants flew around the country conducting focus groups. Exploratory sessions only scratched the surface and failed to fully understand the true business processes. Meanwhile, doubters grew more vocal.

As the program struggled, project sponsors looked for scalps to take rather than heroes to make. A once career-making project became a deathtrap.

Three types of people emerged:
- Peacocks, who wanted fame but not dirty hands
- Naysayers, who wanted to maintain the status quo
- Tiggers (from Winnie the Pooh), who naively expected to "change the world"

Without belaboring the details or assigning blame, it was a mess and a train waiting to derail. Over time, enthusiasm waned as imminent disaster loomed.

Ultimately, the project failed its grand vision. Some components were kept, and through the largesse of corporate accounting, the $100+ million project was written off against an otherwise profitable business.

"Success has many fathers while failure is an orphan."
Tacitus, Agricola 27:1 (98 AD)

Even the greatest company in the world, which GE was at the time, could screw up a major IT transformation project. Only because GE was so otherwise successful could it swallow that scale of the mistake. This pattern was rare for GE but not for the industry at large. Can your company or career survive a similar disaster?

What To Avoid (Case Example #2)

A more recent example involving Intelligent Automation occurred in a large European technology company. The details differ from those of GE, but the project and career results were similar.

The client was excited by the automation opportunity, specifically Robotic Process Automation (RPA), after a consulting firm briefed them on the technology. The proposal process began.

As the consultants began creating a proposal and client negotiations progressed, the process got ugly and pointed to disaster. Key issues included misaligned incentives, role ambiguity, and mismanaged expectations. Hope became the strategy.

Lucrative consulting contracts attract internal volunteers to "help." One group understood Intelligent Automation as having great potential if rolled out gradually across the various parts of the client's business. Their gradual approach would require leadership, communication, change management, aligned incentives, and a long-term focus on achieving value. The other group wanted a huge contract and massive rapid change for the client.

What transpired was a political battle over power, control, and, of course, rewards. The prevailing voice, or "courtier," was a consulting partner of questionable ethics and unquestionable ambition.

The consulting team divided internally as the project careened toward a doomed self-serving approach. Immediately after contract signing, an implementation team arrived on the client site, saying: "We are here to help you eliminate 50 percent of your jobs."

The local manager rewarded for managing a large team naturally felt threatened, became recalcitrant, and the project was soon dead. The project was unrecoverable, and the consulting firm wrote off the entire $20 million contract.

The primary reason for failure was that the incentives and ambitions of a reckless partner were to sell big deals. Working on smaller deals that grew over time did not serve his goals. He was blind to the misalignment in technology, client, circumstances, and timing. Ultimately, this project cost careers and millions of dollars, and sadly could have been avoided.

Lesson From Space

On February 21, 1967, Apollo 1 burned on the launch pad in a horrific loss of life, money, and US prestige.

Failure was caused by hubris and a program recklessly moving forward without effectively evaluating key risks.

This tragedy shook up the system and led to the 1969 success of Apollo 11.

What We Can Learn

These two stories, a large-scale systems integration and Intelligent Automation project, differ in scope but share outcomes. Both are warnings about what can go wrong, yet like NASA's failed early rocket tests, we must press forward to succeed.

What We Want To Emulate

Fortunately, there are wonderful examples of Intelligent Automation success. A simple business we all know something about, fast food, shows a brilliant example of the careful escalation of Intelligent Automation, likely to evolve for many years.

Driving with my wife from Amsterdam to The Hague in 2015, we stopped for lunch. Back then, iPads were new to businesses, yet when we walked into McDonald's, that is what we thought we saw, only bigger. I posted a photo of the touchscreens to US friends labeled as: "the Euro answer to high labor costs and language challenges."

As you likely have experienced, ordering from a touchscreen means you can proceed at your own pace, see what you are ordering, avoid the upsell pressure, and not worry about any language barrier between you and the staff. If you don't want to talk to anyone for any reason, the touchpad is for you.

Roll forward five years, and McDonald's has introduced the screens to 2,500 locations and changed its workforce for good. Think about the benefits and the costs. First, McDonald's can pay a reduced staff more money, and second, it can hire people who don't speak the local language.

As well as reduced cost, there has been a 5 percent sales increase per store in year one with 2 percent each year after that. Going further with Intelligent Automation, McDonald's is rolling out virtual drive-through robots to take your order. Initial tests have been positive for service and cost.[11,12]

Full rollout of Intelligent Automation may include facial recognition and suggested orders based on your prior visits. The system can make you feel special by saying: "Chris, you usually like Dr Pepper; is that what you want today?" or after recognizing two people in the car: "Would you like fries for two?"

This Intelligent Automation implementation is a no-brainer, which explains why many other food outlets have followed suit. Bonus: Somebody's career benefited from this decision, along with the improved service for customers.

The downside for employment means fewer people are hired per store and those who work there get fewer chances to improve their local language, if non-native, reducing future promotion opportunities.

Intelligent Automation can be a career breaker or a career maker, and in many cases, is changing the makeup of workforces in ways like what happened at McDonald's.

However, leading successful automation won't save your career if you fail in other leadership imperatives like ethics, which is exactly what later happened to the CEO of McDonald's when he was publicly fired.[13]

A Cautionary Tale: The Grocer And The Robot

Marianne was a truly wonderful executive assistant who kept our fellow consulting partners on track and organized. She was in her forties and had been doing this type of role for much of her career. She had also graduated from a good college and kept her skills fresh. She was a valuable member of our team and stayed that way. Her husband, I later learned, was in a different situation.

I asked Marianne to join my wife and me for dinner but was disappointed when she declined. She said her husband was "not social" and in a "very dark period" after losing his job. I empathetically asked about his chosen field. He had surprisingly been a grocery clerk working the checkout at a major chain for most of his twenty-five-year career. He had recently been laid off, partly because his union wages continued to grow while his value to the company had flatlined years before.

The grocery store chain had no doubt faced a choice between raising prices on the food it sold to cover rising union wages or ever so gently showing the older employees the door and introducing self-checkout machines. We could debate the policy for hours, including the role of unions, but that's not the point.

The key is that my colleague's husband, like the proverbial frog put into a pot before the heat is turned on, could see and feel the change coming. He saw his younger colleagues with more energy and the ability to scan faster. He saw the one self-checkout machine become two, then three, then six. Still, he failed to act.

If proactive, he would also have seen the rising need for specialists in grocery stores who know unique produce and cheese types, for example, and could have suggested new products being requested by the younger customers. In short, he could have found ways to add more value to the store, but instead, like the frog, he failed to move until it was too late.

My friend's husband likely knew part of the problem was his hesitancy to act. He likely spent months blaming other people, outside events, or the world for his plight. We never did have dinner with my colleague and her husband because he never did get over his state of mind.

The Solution Is Noble Automation

It doesn't have to be this way; our colleagues do not need to sit in water like a frog waiting for something to happen. We can lead the way to ever-improving businesses with jobs that require more and more of our innately human skills, feelings, insights, and energy. We can do this by looking for and chasing down ways to increase value for others while improving our own lives. The grocer could have been proactive about his career and value to the company, and his leader could have helped. The solution is not just Intelligent Automation; the solution is Noble Automation.

Noble Automation Realized

Noble Automation, as used in this book, is the combination of applying Intelligent Automation and inspired leadership that focuses on maximizing the positive outcomes for all stakeholders. These include the shareholder, the employee, the leaders, and the community. Noble Automation actively seeks to make work an adventure that grows both people and profits.

The benefits of implementing Noble Automation include freeing people to be more human by removing drudgery, providing insights, and allowing us the time and energy to feel, think, empathize, and connect. It means profitably putting the full value of human ingenuity to work.

The next chapter is a quick run-through of how.

Noble Automation Means Keeping Technology Beneficial

"Everything we love about civilization is a product of intelligence, so amplifying our human intelligence with artificial intelligence has the potential of helping civilization flourish like never before— as long as we manage to keep the technology beneficial."[14]

Max Tegmark, President of the Future of Life Institute

PART TWO
Accelerate Innovation, Motivation And
Growth With Noble Automation

*"What makes excellence? To turn the present
circumstances to your advantage."*
Pittacus of Mytilene, one of the Seven Sages of Greece

That uneasy feeling you may have about your business and career when you hear about artificial intelligence and automation is not just you. These technologies and the rest of what has been called the Fourth Industrial Revolution represent a huge opportunity and an existential threat mixed into a cloud of hype and blather.

So, how do you figure out what is happening and what you can do? Here is a three-sentence version of a recommended approach:
1. Automation is here, and we need to use it to survive as a business, but...
2. We don't know exactly what to do with automation, and we are afraid we will scare off or alienate our best people in the process.
3. We need to know how best to implement these powerful emerging capabilities to innovate, remain competitive, and retain top talent.

The Situation, Complication, And Key Question For Noble Automation

The above pattern is one of the most powerful yet seemingly simple techniques to approach any business problem. The idea was advanced by Barbara Minto in her book, *The Pyramid Principle*.[15] This framework forms the backbone of many effective strategy projects delivered to world-class companies.

The approach distilled breaks the problem into three pieces before proposing solutions.

The three steps are often referred to as:
1. The Situation
2. The Complication
3. The Key Question

The Situation is a selection of facts describing the specific challenge faced by the organization. These facts include how your company is performing, the number of products you sell, the financial metrics of your business, and the demographics of the company or market. The situation includes what the company is trying to achieve. For example, "Company X wants to grow by 20 percent in the next eighteen months" is a fact and key part of the situation. Only facts and relevant details with a direct impact on the overall problem to solve are included.

The Complication is a list of whatever is preventing the company from achieving its goals. These are both factual and subjective points. For example, "Company X wants to grow by 20 percent in eighteen months but does not have the skilled workers to deliver that revenue." Other points may be "Company X's competitors are producing better products or services." The point is to capture what is getting in the way of success.

The Key Question is the single question that, if answered, will help you achieve your goals. For example, "What new product or service can Company X bring to market in the next six months to help you achieve your growth goals?" Stating a key question is difficult because it forces the company to focus on one key question when many ideas are likely competing for attention. The key question is important because without it being specific, there is no clarity on what the business is trying to do. This degrades momentum and morale.

These three points lead to the executive's priority—specifically, the proposed solution.

The Proposed Solution results from weighing viable options to address the key question. While a mathematically driven solution with measurable facts and scientific proof would certainly eliminate debate, the reality is that most solutions will be educated guesses.

By educated guess, the people who come together to do projects like these collect as much information as possible to support various options. Since any given problem could require endless data and consume enormous amounts of time, choosing the most indicative data available is essential. The team then relies on its industry or problem expertise to complement the data and support a recommended course of action.

The best thinkers collect what information is needed and mix it with what they and their clients or colleagues already know.

The team combines this information, weighs the options, then hopefully proposes a good solution. A good solution is imperfect but has a strong chance of working. Over time, you may need changes.

So, with that background, below are the situation, complication, and key question facing many companies today.

The Intelligent Automation Situation

The world is global, and ideas, people, goods, and services flow more easily than ever before. The business implications are profound and present both opportunities and risks. Intelligent Automation is a powerful combination of tools that many business leaders want to use to improve performance.

Transformations of processes and business models have been an important aspect of business success for many years. With the new technologies available today, these transformations can happen much faster. Companies can do this themselves or watch industry disrupters do it to them. The breadth and depth of automation's impact contribute to the scale and speed of disruption.

What is available today to business leaders or startups is a combination of new technologies, big data, massive cloud processing power, and globalized talent. The new technologies are easier to connect to than previous generations of tech. Big data makes finding patterns much simpler. Massive cloud processing makes computing cheaper, and the globalized talent pool means the right person can do the work at the right price. All of this is an opportunity that business leaders want to capture to avoid an equally great threat of job loss and fear.

Automation is commonly mentioned in the press with the usual mix of hype and reality. Several studies suggest a huge threat to a range of jobs, including truck driving, cashiers, clerks, lawyers, stockbrokers, and customer service agents.

Situation Big Picture:

- Executives want to keep the jobs they have earned.
- Leaders want to save their business, company, and in some cases, country.
- Competition for most companies is global.
- Workforces are mobile and virtual.
- Some jobs will go away.
- IT skills are both more valuable and pricier than ever.
- Legacy systems from ERPs to desktop spreadsheets and specialty tools like Salesforce and Workday are not adequately integrated.
- Humans spend hours at work on tasks better handled by machines.
- Humans spend too little time doing what humans do best.
- Disruptors are looking to unseat any established business with technology.
- Many employees are disengaged, becoming effectively untapped resources when they are needed most.

Situation For Employee Engagement:

- Only 15 percent of employees are engaged with their company and job; 33 percent are looking for another job.[16]
- 71 percent of CEOs say employee engagement is critical to their company's success.[17]
- 69 percent of employees say they would work harder if they felt appreciated.
- High employee engagement firms are 21 percent more profitable.[18]
- 81 percent of employees are considering leaving their job.[19]
- 74 percent of millennials would accept a pay cut for their ideal job.[20]

The Intelligent Automation Complications

Despite the desire to employ Intelligent Automation, many leaders are failing to achieve the desired results. Some are failing to start due to overwhelm, fear, lack of support, etc. For others, automation means throwing huge resources at the problem without a clear plan. Some have started but got stuck midway. Complications are not created equal, and many are red herrings or distractions.

Leaders are paid to act in uncertain and demanding environments, so act they do, and the outcome can be negative because of inadequate appreciation for the unintended consequences. Of course, the negatives of not acting can be severe as well.

The earlier example about the CFO who announced half his team would lose their jobs highlights one of the biggest complications. The CFO had planned the overall message. The message was like many of those said by other C-suite executives in Europe and North America. The difference in this case was that he said it to the room full of people who would be impacted by the goal, with little detailed explanation about how it would affect everyone. Intelligent Automation may get deployed but not Noble Automation.

The tragedy here is that messages like these are delivered with generally the same effect worldwide. This CFO is no idiot and certainly does not have diminished mental capacity. He is quite bright and successful. He does, however, have a blind spot.

What he was doing is what many of us do when we are under enormous pressure to perform. A form of tunnel vision sets in that blocks out anything but the direct path to a specific goal. The mistake appears in the unintended consequences to which we were blind at the time. So why would any similarly talented executive behave like this?

Five Common Reasons For Failing To Succeed With Automation

Ignorance of the options: Many leaders are simply unaware of what can be done with the tools of Intelligent Automation. You can't drive what you don't understand.

Pressure to act: Executives and department leaders are all under relentless pressure to improve their business. Automation is a hot term and, therefore, many of these leaders feel the need to "do something."

Mixed messages: Employees desperately listen for clear and consistent messaging. When it is absent, the biggest symptom is stalled progress.

Misaligned incentives: If personal incentives do not support applying automation technologies at the leadership level or below, complications manifest, progress does not.

Employee disengagement: Implementing Intelligent Automation is an all-hands-on-deck journey. Employees who are not engaged will prevent progress. Two big drivers of this are a clear purpose that connects the individual and company success and too much mundane work that numbs people's minds. Younger employees are likely to respond by leaving.

Complications Summary:

- Many leaders do not know what to do with Intelligent Automation.
- Some act too slowly and some act too fast—both extremes produce problems.
- Too often, all stakeholders are not considered.
- Frequently, incentives are misaligned within the company.
- Any combination of the above leads to employee disengagement.
- Part of the disengagement comes from a lack of overall stated compelling purpose.
- Many employees are terrified of losing their jobs.
- Millennial talent votes with their feet.

The Intelligent Automation Key Question

After you and your team review, edit, and add to the above points for the situation and complications, you will be in a better position to narrow your focus to one key question.

Your key question must fit your company and consider what you have already done with automation. Here is a version to consider.

Key Question (Sample)
What business areas would benefit most from these new technologies, and how do we assemble, motivate, and reward the right people to execute the plan, deliver an attractive ROI, and retain our best performers?

The Recommended Solution: Employ Noble Automation

The recommended solution for the above key question has three options:
1. Internally shape a plan to embark on or accelerate Noble Automation.
2. Outsource the planning to a consulting company to do it for you.
3. Partner with outside consultants to help you create a plan that leverages your business knowledge and their subject matter expertise.

There are tradeoffs and best practices for doing any of these options outside of this book's scope. However, to avoid leaving you hanging, you may want to consider these questions:

- Do you have the internal resources who can formulate this plan and do their current jobs?

- Will your company listen to internal experts, or do they need to hear from someone outside the walls of your firm?

- Do you think a broader view is currently necessary?

- Can you work collaboratively with outsider professionals and balance the accountability/responsibility required for long-term success?

NOBLE AUTOMATION NOW METHOD - SEVEN ESSENTIALS

RESULTS

7 : ALIGNED INCENTIVES AND CULTURE

6 : OPERATING MODEL BUILT FOR PURPOSE

5 : HELPING HUMANS BE HEROES

4 : EMPOWERED & EXCITED TEAMS

3 : A FOCUS ON VALUE CREATION

2 : UNDERSTANDING THE TECHNOLOGY

1 : INSPIRED AND INFORMED LEADERSHIP

TIME

Whichever approach you choose, this book is written to help you frame this for yourself, as the executive in charge or the person executing the plan.

The remainder of this book completes the Noble Automation Now Method. It is the product of years of expensive and painful trial and error that you can skip by applying it yourself (see the chart):

Noble Automation Now Methodology Summary:

1. Leaders who can improve their businesses holistically and inspire the adoption of change and technology implementation

2. A sufficiently deep and broad understanding of the new technologies in both leaders and team members

3. A clear path to focus on value and avoid being distracted by office politics, white elephants, or shiny new technology

4. An excited and empowered team with the tools, knowledge, and support it needs to succeed

5. Humans who are helped to see that they can be heroes in your business and their own lives

6. An operating model that combines people, process, and technology to deliver value, delight customers, and satisfy employees and shareholders

7. Incentives, tangible (financial) and intangible (what gets praise and attention), aligned to deliver the desired outcomes

An Inspiring Success Story—Noble Automation In Action

A European finance company I worked with approached automation differently and achieved noble results. The story highlights:

The company CEO recognized the potential of automation and empowered Jens, a young director, to explore the range of options. While the CEO's automation knowledge was shallow, his support for Jens was deep.

Jens located industry experts to educate him and his deputies on Noble Automation. These education sessions included technology, business operating models, industry use cases, and recognizing potential conflicts of interest between consulting firms and technology choices. With his raised awareness, Jens was better able to shape the overall automation direction.

He also made sure his superiors were well informed, comfortable, and willing to support the plan. To do this, the director met privately with the leadership team members to help them understand the technology and business possibilities. In return, the leadership team helped Jens see hidden roadblocks, including political considerations, and identify communication strategies that would best promote success. The result was consensus and leadership support.

Jens then identified potential team members from various functional areas likely to be involved in the project. He lobbied the senior leaders for the best team members rather than the readily available or *expendable* people.

Working closely with HR, he ensured each team member's performance would be evaluated and their success recognized when the project finished. Clear expectations and the definition of success excited and motivated the team.

To draw out his team's full potential, Jens arranged for just-in-time training on the key technologies and methods. His senior leadership approved the training budgets and kept the team moving smoothly.

As the project progressed, team members worked closely on the shared goal while simultaneously moving forward on their professional journeys. Jens worked with each team member to think through long-term personal opportunities made possible from working on the project. Each member could see how succeeding in the project and changing the business would allow them to thrive inside the transformed company or outside with new skills and knowledge.

With the team aligned on a shared goal and vividly aware of the personal implications, they were free to build a new and effective business model. They story-boarded the future business and role-played how the changes would affect the company. They uncovered what would work versus what sounded good on paper. The team architected a process and model they would want to live in and work with.

Finally, in close partnership with the HR and executive teams, the project team suggested what ideal behaviors they saw going forward and how these would support the business's needs. The HR team crafted and aligned the tangible and intangible personal incentives across the affected areas of the company.

When the first wave of Noble Automation was complete, the team paid careful attention to the future-facing messaging. Specifically, this was the first wave of a steady and endless journey to keep the company competitive in the market and reward the employees who worked there.

This project team successfully achieved Noble Automation by focusing on the business's success and to the maximum extent possible—all the stakeholders.

The next seven steps are a roadmap you may want to use in your journey to successful Noble Automation.

Summary

- The situation today includes a compelling need to implement automation and AI in significant parts of our businesses.

- Time is running out for some companies as competitors and labor market pressure grow.

- Complicating this goal is a lack of knowledge and experience in effectively implementing this basket of technology with today's workforce.

- This knowledge gap is in the technology, applying it, and getting the best out of our teams in the process.

- There are many epic failed attempts with wasted time, money, and goodwill. Fortunately, there are also examples of inspiring success. We can understand the differences.

- The solution is Noble Automation, which uses the technology to profitably serve all stakeholders.

- Noble Automation is a philosophical approach and a basket of tools and methods that have proven successful for leading companies. You can learn and leverage these tools to succeed.

- The benefits of Noble Automation include freeing people to be more human by removing drudgery, providing insights, and allowing us the time and energy to feel, think, empathize, and connect.

NOBLE AUTOMATION NOW
Seven Steps

2 : UNDERSTANDING THE TECHNOLOGY

1 : INSPIRED AND INFORMED LEADERSHIP

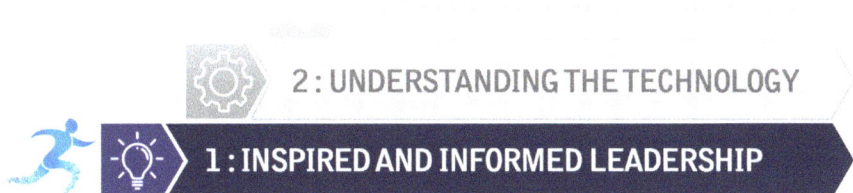

Step One—Inspired And Informed Leadership

"Leaders are the people who bring out our best while making us believe we could have done it ourselves." [21]
William Conaty, **Former GE Chief Human Resources Officer**

The Pacific Ocean is immense and beyond what humans can accurately visualize. It is four times wider than the United States, where few have even driven from coast to coast. From across the Pacific, winds can blow for days, resulting in epic storms. My fellow San Diego residents rarely saw those storms, but we benefited from the waves reaching the shore.

Waves come in sets of five to seven, and usually, but not always, the last wave is the biggest. [22] The first few waves serve as a wake-up call for surfers. They never know how many waves are in the set, so they must choose which to catch. When the best wave passes, there still may be smaller echo waves but with less potential for excitement.

As a body or board surfer, we know to wait for the later waves if we want the biggest ride. We also know that preparation makes all the difference. In the ocean, being ready means positioning yourself at the right distance from the shore and having the energy to take advantage of the wave when it arrives. Wait too far out, and the wave will have an insufficient shape to carry you. Wait too close to shore, and the wave will crash on your head.

Finally, if you stay out in the ocean, waiting for the perfect wave, it may never arrive. If it does, you may be too tired to catch it. Riding great waves is exciting and about balance, timing, preparation, and simply being in the water. It is all about choice.

Business, in many ways, is like the ocean. It is vast and filled with uncertainty and sunny and stormy days. The thrill comes from the challenging days, and in business, those are days of change and innovation. Intelligent Automation started as a wave far away from most businesses, and like the ocean waves, it is accompanied by preceding waves and will be followed by lagging "echo" waves.

Those of us in business are in the ocean at various distances from the shore. The early waves have come and crashed on the beach. The big wave, the one where all the glory will be, is still far enough offshore to be able to adjust our position. One event is certain: the wave is coming, and there are only two ways to avoid it.

As in the ocean, if you want to avoid a wave, you can swim way out deep, where the swell will gently pass under you. By doing this, you will never have the thrill of the ride or the business change. If you stay out too long, letting the swells pass, you will eventually paddle back into a changed world where your friends have gone home. In business, if you wait too long, you may no longer be competitive or relevant.

You can also avoid the wave by leaving the sea (business) altogether. Let's assume you are reading this book because you want to stay in the water and experience at least one more big wave and maybe many more.

Not everyone in your company will share your thirst for adventure and excitement and will likely find waves of change unsettling. So, to get your colleagues and teammates to come along for the ride, you need to lead. The first step is to help others see what is coming and feel confident enough to stay in the ocean, wait for the wave, and kick hard when the time comes.

Noble Automation, the most recent big wave, is the collective term we are using to describe a basket of technologies and inspired leadership available for businesses today. You, as the leader of a small or large team, need to have a clear idea of where to use these tools, their purpose, and the most important problem or opportunity to address. Without these, you might build something that doesn't help your business.

Figure 1 Photo Credit: Winchester Mystery House®

A Winchester Lesson

Consider the Winchester Mystery House in San Jose, California, the estate of the late Sarah Winchester, heiress to the Winchester Repeating Arms Company, founded by Oliver Winchester. The house is a great counter testament to planning and tool use.

Sarah Winchester was inspired to change, that's for sure. Unfortunately, like a business leader led astray by an unethical or incompetent consultant or enamored with growth for growth's sake, Ms. Winchester listened to a mystic who persuaded her to keep building or she would go to hell; so, build she did according to the legend.

The result was a house with roughly 161 rooms, including forty bedrooms, two ballrooms, forty-seven fireplaces, 10,000 panes of glass, and seventeen chimneys, all built at great expense and with no rhyme or reason. Rooms did not follow a plan, and some hallways led to nowhere with doors opening to walls. Clearly, anyone outside could see that some form of craziness was involved here, yet Sarah Winchester was viewed as a social icon with unique eccentricities and an impressive house. This is not unlike some short-term successful executives.

We can likely agree that to create a comfortable home to both live in and entertain, a plan would have helped. Instead, she had no concept of how the building would function. "Just keep building," is what she reputedly said.

The house now stands as a local curio and kitschy attraction. My fear for many businesspeople is that their companies or careers could go the way of the Winchester Mystery House rather than the way of an elegantly designed building with purpose, style, efficiency, and respect. Because overcomplicated, poorly designed businesses don't become tourist attractions—they disappear.

Instead, Be Like Frank

Frank Lloyd Wright had a vision to build an entire school of building design he called organic architecture. He also aspired to be a great and respected leader. As with building great companies or teams, Wright committed to and followed consistent principles in the various buildings he created.

He knew that each client would be different, and each site would require adjustments, but each would benefit from consistent principles of good design, order, and construction. The results included some of the most recognizable and praised homes ever built. (See Figure 2)

Figure 2 Photo Credit: T.S. Long—Robie House built 1910

Wright learned to balance the combination of overarching principles with the specific demands of unique lots and customers. As a leader he holistically understood his craft and the environment. When you see a Wright house, you can feel the way it comes together like a well-run company feels when you are in it.

Just as Wright was necessary to build his historical and functional homes, you as the leader are necessary to lead your future business or function, and you must do it based on principles balanced with the needs of the specific company and team.

Most importantly, you have the position to make or suggest these changes and you have access to the combined resources, people, authority, and rewards to make it happen. You are the architect. So, what kind of business do you want to build?

It is the principled approach of Wright rather than the scattered approach of Sarah Winchester that hopefully inspires you as you look at the collection of tools we call Noble Automation and use them well to lead a company or department to be proud of.

What Is A Great Company?

This is not the first time the question has been asked. The last time national focus was applied to this question was in the 1980s, when the Japanese basically ruled the world with top-quality companies and products. In the eighties, the Japanese were the inspiration to the business world.

In response to the perceived threat to American industry, the US formed a commission to study the problem and the opportunity. Rarely do such commissions produce meaningful results, but in this case, they produced the Malcolm Baldrige National Quality Award. It is an impressive, well-thought-out, and achievable plan for a business.

Winners of the Baldrige Award must demonstrate high degrees of holistic competence across their business. Over the last twenty-five years, winners have included some of America's best-run companies, measured by financial success and how they treated their people and communities.

While the full depth of this award is beyond the focus of this book, the criteria for winning the award is fully complementary to how successful companies implement Noble Automation.

A Note Of Caution About Certificates And Awards

Caution is wise with awards, certifications, and qualifications. Some well-meaning businesspeople lose sight of the business and begin to focus on awards and certifications. This is common with business excellence, quality, lean, and ISO.

As a General Electric (GE) Six Sigma Master Black Belt, I repeatedly saw quality people obsessed with the specific criteria for Six Sigma projects. This obsession leads to projects being held back because of some arcane statistical measure tangential to business outcomes. This demotivates teams and delays results.

If the high priests of quality, or whatever other certification, are left to their own devices, the business will suffer, and the usefulness of the methodology with be tarnished. The point of any certification or award like Baldrige is to improve the business, not slavishly following the letter of the criteria, especially when doing so leads to high project costs or long delays.

"One should practice much sense, not much learning."
Periander, ancient Corinthian leader

Reading the Baldrige Award criteria and concluding this is too much to tackle would also be a mistake. Instead, be the elephant eater who takes one bite at a time or the marathon runner who starts with the first step. Both cliches translated to incremental action will lead to steady success over time.

Below is a quick summary of the criteria. In the leadership deep dive (Appendix A) are diamonds with useful and detailed examples of applying them to your business, including specific points from prominent and successful CEOs and chief human resources officers.

The Baldrige Award: A Recipe For A Great Company With A Great Leader

According to Baldrige, great companies must compare favorably on eleven holistic criteria. They must show strength across the metrics that benefit employees, shareholders, and the community. These criteria, created before the current wave of social activism, show that great companies and great leaders focus on broad positively reinforcing dimensions that ultimately result in business success.

Baldrige Award Criteria Summary[23]

Systems perspective	Thinking and leading the interconnected parts of your business
Visionary leadership	Having a vision that is clear and compelling to the whole company
Customer-focused excellence	Keeping the focus on the people who pay for your goods and services
Valuing people	Genuinely recognizing the value and dignity of your colleagues
Organizational learning and agility	Consciously and deliberately developing people and making changes at market speed
Focus on success	This success is multi-dimensional and clearly defined
Managing for innovation	Balancing the value of the proven with the necessity of the new
Management by fact	Facts as compared to politics or emotion
Societal responsibility	Having a measurable positive impact on the larger society in which you operate
Ethics and transparency	Being open, honest, and clear
Delivering value and results	The last and most important point is to succeed in delivering value and results

The Baldrige criteria is a robust approach to building a successful company, but it could obscure the personal leadership style and actions most important to success with Noble Automation.

Let's focus on the most common and crippling behaviors and beliefs of leaders who fail with Intelligent Automation. These evolve from the details of the Baldrige criteria.

The Top Five Leadership Barriers For Successful Noble Automation

Barriers To Success	Ways To Overcome Them
Ignorance of options	Learn the art of the possible
Pressure to act now	Begin with proofs of concept
Mixed messages	Demonstrate your clear commitment
Engagement and the purpose of work	Be the voice of inspiration
Misaligned incentives	Call them out and fix them

Ignorance Of (Automation) Options

Many leaders are unaware of their options or lack an understanding of which options are most promising and have the least chance of collateral damage. Cost-cutting is the most direct short-term path to improved performance. If leaders are unaware of growth or innovation options, they will act on what they know.

Cost-cutting comes in many forms, including outsourcing, downsizing, and now automation. Cost-cutting doesn't generally increase revenues unless the cutting can be transferred to lower prices and more sales. Most importantly, cost-cutting does not innovate the products or services and often leads to a race for the bottom. Leaders are often unaware of the options that can generate revenue through creative innovation.

The data is clear on what best supports long-term business success for most companies, and cost-cutting takes a backseat to growth through revenue generation and margin improvement via innovation. Yet the cost-cutting continues because the pressure is only getting worse. The point was likely on the mind of the previously mentioned CFO.

Many of today's Noble Automation options can lead directly to growth by capturing data, suggesting actions, and enabling employees to direct clients to additional sales. These options will be missed if your team only believes they are trying to cut costs.

To lead effectively with Noble Automation, leaders need to know what is possible in enough detail to be the champion of change. This is solved through education, and this book is a good start to that process. Step 2 will do a quick run-through of the technologies and how they can solve business problems and grow revenue.

Pressure To Act

Pressure in a closed container or a business enterprise usually leads to escape through the path of least resistance. In business, that often looks like cost-cutting and drastic measures like outsourcing. If executives are under the kind of pressure that prevents them from thinking more clearly and more holistically, they will act on short-term fixes.

The pressure to act often builds when some new buzzword or idea becomes the obsession of the boss or the stock analysts. When a phrase like artificial intelligence becomes a leadership buzzword, the pressure to act feels unavoidable.

When a leader hasn't been proactive with a plan that deals with a new buzzword, a likely scenario emerges. This is when the leader says to his boss something like: "We are all over that and will have a formal plan for you shortly."

Unfortunately, the approach is all too common. Junior leaders can be particularly hesitant to admit being caught off guard. When asked by the boss, they often tap dance about how they have been working on the hot new thing.

If they get away with it, they often do some impulsive project that is poorly planned out, under-delivers, and inoculates that part of the organization from the new technology. Does this sound familiar?

What is a leader to do when caught flat-footed about the potential of automation? Perhaps say to the boss: "If you agree that this Intelligent Automation idea may have potential for us, how about we do a proof of concept on a part of the business, build excitement and knowledge, and then grow from there? If successful, I will bring you a plan for taking it to scale to move the performance needle." Most senior executives would be happy to hear the ambition and the humility in this statement.

Mixed Messages

In Jack Welch's last five years as GE CEO, I heard him talk unforgettably about messaging. Jack (he expected us to call him Jack) said:

> *"I know when I have said something enough times when the audience can repeat it for me and not before."* [24]

I heard the former chairman of Cisco, John Chambers, echo this. Jack and Chambers knew that companies and any organization listen little to leadership unless the message is clear, consistent, and repeated. If you are not almost sick of saying the same thing, you have likely not yet convinced your company or your team that you mean it.

In contrast, I worked at GE when Jeff Immelt took over. We sat in a room with fifty other young executives as the new chairman told us his priorities. While we could not predict that Immelt would struggle so much with leading GE and that 9/11 would decimate the aircraft engine business, we could suspect that he would struggle to get his message across.

He spoke for more than an hour, and we could not tell you what his top priorities were. Instead, he walked through a litany of items with no clear ranking. When Jack spoke, everyone in the room knew his top three priorities. It was quite a contrast in style and results.

The Most Powerful Tools: Engagement And The Purpose Of Work

Employee engagement describes people caring enough about their jobs that they apply their full attention and effort. Engagement is easier to measure when your employees are manufacturing items. Tolerances can be checked, and quality can be verified. Managers can tell themselves that since their parts are okay, their employees are "engaged." If your manufacturing employees want to screw over the company or don't care about their jobs, the reality quickly shows up in poor quality products.

One of my favorite examples of employee disengagement was the manufacturing "employees" of Oskar Schindler in World War II. You may remember from the movie that Schindler was the German industrialist, sympathetic to the plight of the Jews, who bought the lives of his Jewish employees away from the German death camps to ostensibly make war materials and other products.

Schindler saved the lives of more than one thousand employees by telling the Nazis that he needed them for his industrial plants making armaments and other items for the German military. He then went on to be the least engaged manager of the least engaged employees in history, making defective armaments.

This is a great example of how truly capable people can completely undermine your business if they don't subscribe to the company's mission. Despite the potential to offend, this is a great story because it is so visceral and raw. We cheered when in the movie we learned that Schindler's Jews made the goods crappy on purpose. Brilliant.

What about the rest of us not being forced to make armaments for the enemy? How can we measure a person only giving us half of what they could? This is where the situation gets complicated for two reasons. The first is purpose, and the second is the type of work millions of people do today.

Purpose: Truly effective leaders regularly reinforce the organization's purpose and connect that to the individual jobs as a compelling reason to come to work.

For example, the best financial services leaders say something like this:

"We come to work every day to evaluate and process loans to businesses in the healthcare industry so that they can provide the kind of care their patients want and deserve. Our capital allows people to be healthier and live better lives, which, in turn, makes our whole community a better place to live."

If all the company talks about is growth, profit, and net income, the message is loud and clear. What is valued at the company is money and the purpose is to make more of it.

I am not naive and rather fully understand that many companies are populated with people who *only* care about profit. Profit is also the only reason the company remains in business. Those companies will never capture the hearts and minds of their employees, which eventually leads to a different culture. A money-only culture will only attract a certain kind of person.

Type of Work: Despite all the technology we have at our disposal today, millions of people still do mind-numbing and uninspiring work. This is demotivating at the core.

The assembly line took farmworkers from the fields and increased their standard of living. Routine assembly work paid more but was boring and has steadily been replaced by mechanization and automation. Similarly, knowledge work too often means people sitting at computers doing boring work and not connecting that work to the company's larger purpose.

The challenge we have as leaders, if we want the most engagement possible, is to improve the quality and challenge of the work our colleagues do. That is, to make it more suitable for humans.

Having a clear and inspirational work purpose is to a company like general physical fitness is to a human body. It is tough to pinpoint the specific exercise that made you nimble and strong, but you know when it happens. A clear purpose makes the whole business nimbler and stronger.

Watching the highly regarded film *Citizen Kane* one night, a point on the power of purpose jumped out. The film, if you haven't seen it, is quasi-biographical about a recently deceased multi-billionaire. Kane, the billionaire, was a complicated figure and lived a life of fame and notoriety. His dying word is "rosebud," leaving the world to ponder its meaning. A newspaper reporter sees this as his hook for an exposé on the enigmatic business titan.

The reporter was impressed by Kane's money-making capabilities and tracked down Kane's former business manager to ask Kane's secret. The reporter suggested Kane must have had some incredible talent to make himself so rich. The former business manager replies:

> *"Well, it's no trick to make a lot of money*
> *if all you want to do is make a lot of money."*
> ***Citizen Kane*** **(1941)**[25]

This primary motivation of making money may work for some, but today, millennials especially are looking for a purpose beyond money to motivate them. Many millennials don't want to own things and instead want to accumulate experiences.

Strategically, leaders need to communicate the company's higher purpose if they want to tap into the higher potential of their teams. Here are a few examples from successful leaders.

Industry Examples Of The Purpose Of Work

Healthcare:

Uninspired   Our purpose is to provide healthcare.

More Inspired: Our purpose is to help others improve their health and live more meaningful and rewarding lives.

Financial services:

Uninspired   Our purpose is to grow the company and make more money.

More Inspired: Our purpose is to be the lubrication in a free-market economy, facilitating companies big and small that provide valuable products and services to the communities where we, too, live.

Insurance:

Uninspired   Our purpose is to insure people against losses in their personal and professional lives.

More Inspired: Our purpose is to remove stress from people's minds so that they can live more fulfilled and focus on what matters most to them, like friends, family, and professional growth.

Restaurants:

Uninspired   Our purpose is to make good food and get return customers

More Inspired: Our purpose is to provide an experience where people can recharge their bodies with nutritional food and recharge their spirits with lively conversation.

Finally, my favorite story about the power of purpose:

A young man announced to his friend that he was leaving his Midwestern town and its bucolic farming industry to join the exciting circus life. Reluctantly, his friends and family accepted his decision and bid him farewell.

Months later, after receiving letters recounting her friend's new life of excitement, a young ranch hand went to see her former colleague at the visiting circus.

Sitting in the stands in her best overalls, she saw her friend walking behind the elephants, shoveling up their dung with a big smile on his face.

When the show was over, the friends reunited. After exchanging hugs, the ranch hand asked: "I saw you behind the elephants. That looks like a terrible job and just like cleaning stalls on the farm. Why don't you quit?"

Her friend looked back, paused, and then adamantly replied, "What, and quit show business?"

If your employees don't see a clear and inspiring purpose for your company and their jobs, they will resort to what they know for sure: it pays the bills.

To tap into the full potential of your employees, teams, and fellow executives, you need a reason to be doing what you are doing that inspires. You need your version of "show business." Too many companies and leaders lack this compelling purpose and suffer reduced employee engagement as a result.

Misaligned Incentives

Charlie Munger, vice chairman of Berkshire Hathaway, says it best: "Show me the incentives and I will show you the outcome."[26]

Incentives are the subject of a vast volume of research but in essence are clear. The big point here is simple—your incentives are misaligned, and you will likely struggle when you tell someone to do one thing and reward them for something else.

A common example is to tell a leader that they should have the best possible team for the job and then only reward them for a low-cost structure. This is a classic case of incentive misalignment. Incentive misalignment is all too common and partly due to adopting a "hope and change" mentality. That is, "hope" that unintended consequences will not be a problem and that only positive "changes" will happen.

This approach is far too frequent and amplified because many organizations openly know that their leaders have conflicting incentives, yet the board or C-suite throw up their hands, saying it is too hard to fix.

Misaligned incentives, in the best case, cause conflict and sub-optimal work. In the worst case, people lose respect for their leaders and organization. This decreases engagement and increases employee turnover.

The solution is to think through what you want to happen, storyboard how the business works, and align the company and individual incentives to reward your ideal outcome. Systems thinking is a helpful discipline here. *The Fifth Discipline* by Peter Senge brought systems thinking out of the lab and into the executive suite.

When executives say things like, "We know there is significant conflict in the incentives, but we expect people to act like professionals and do the right thing," that is a sure sign of lazy, non-systems based, or wishful thinking.

Summary: Noble Automation Now Method Step One

- The waves of Intelligent Automation are rolling in like the waves of the sea.

- Companies will be washed away unless they have leaders who embrace the technology and set a clear vision for adopting it for the firm.

- Leading a great company is like creating a philosophy for architecture. They both require principles that can be honed and repeated.

- A good North Star for leadership has been established by the Malcolm Baldrige Quality Award.

- Most companies and leaders can benefit from referring to the Baldrige criteria.

- Specific to Noble Automation, some emerging highly supportive behaviors for leaders to consider:

  1. Knowing your options

  2. Resisting pressure to act (without planning)

  3. Sending clear messages

  4. Celebrating the purpose of work

  5. Aligning incentives

The second step in the Noble Automation Now Method is to understand the technology, which we will do next.

2 : UNDERSTANDING THE TECHNOLOGY

Step Two—Understanding the Technology

Understanding the technology of Noble Automation is like understanding the various tools in Home Depot (DIY store) or Williams Sonoma (cooking store).

In both stores, you can occasionally see demonstrations of various new tools or those that are unique in their approach to known challenges. Noble Automation is analogous to these. As with a new power saw or crepe maker, you don't get excited unless you want or need them. You at least need to justify a need to your husband or wife. Oh, the power tools spouses have bought this way.

When walking into one of the above stores, you likely think, *I want to . . .*

Home Depot Needs	Williams Sonoma Needs
Cut something	Cut something
Paint something	Cook something
Join things	Make something
Dig/fill	Blend something
Learn something	Present something
Build something	Measure something

Needs for the Intelligent Automation "store":

Move something	Take information or physical items from one place and put them somewhere else
Calculate something	Add, subtract, multiply, and divide numbers based on specific rules
Decide something	Evaluate information and make a decision, e.g. go left, cancel, flag it, approve it, deny it, etc.
Change something	Add information, change a color, insert or delete words
Recognize something	Compare words, images, or sounds against known definitions and label those items
Create or transform something	Assemble various pieces and create a new object
Interpret one or many things	Evaluate ambiguous words, actions, or patterns and choose what they likely mean or imply
Follow instructions	Do specific steps in a particular order following rules

From this list, we can talk about the various tools, technologies, and supporting infrastructure that make up Intelligent Automation.

The tools fall into four technology categories:

• A *doer* executes a task on one or more systems.

• A *decider* takes in various inputs, decides the output, and determines what should be done with it.

• A *learner or thinker* consumes data and provides insights into that data. Over time, it can anticipate and eventually suggest optimal paths to take.

• A *mover* is a robot or machine that physically moves something.

The table below includes *some* of the technologies currently included in Intelligent Automation. This is an imperfect guide. First, the field is growing quickly, and new tools come along frequently. Second, there are different interpretations of what should be included in Intelligent Automation. The tools solve specific problems. Together, they create Intelligent Automation solutions.

Intelligent Automation Tools

Technology Types	Specific Examples
Do	Robotic process automation (unattended)
	Robotic process automation (attended)
	Chatbots
	Virtual assistants
	Workflow tools
	Business process management (BPM)
	Physical robot (mover)
Decide	Image recognition
	Natural language processing
Learn/Think	Conversational artificial intelligence
	Machine learning
	Cognitive computing/agents
	Artificial intelligence

The Intelligent Automation tools are in some ways like Lego bricks. In practice you may want to build Fallingwater from Legos, but to do so, you need to understand how to use the individual bricks. Once you know what each brick can do, you can go back to the plans and create a variety of buildings. Once you know what the Noble Automation tools can do, you can build many potential solutions.

Figure 3 LEGO® brick

For example, you can use RPA (Robotic Process Automation) to open an email, extract information, and move that content to another system. That is a powerful building block. Now that you know what RPA does, you can work it into your plan.

Figure 4 Architecture Fallingwater.
Photos used with permission.
©2021 The LEGO Group

The following summarizes the above tools to give you a running start at knowing what is out there and what they do.

45

Robotic Process Automation (Unattended)

Robotic Process Automation (RPA) is software that mimics a person sitting at a workstation, likely using multiple systems and completing rules-based tasks. The software robot follows the rules and executes the tasks across systems at high speed and with no errors. Tasks assigned to RPA are generally repetitive, data-entry heavy, rules-based, and fraught with wasted time maneuvering between screens and systems. The term unattended means the robot takes a batch of information and executes it from start to stop without involving humans.

A Caution On Creating New Tools

You can build amazing Intelligent Automation solutions without creating new technologies and tools.

Beware the team that first wants to write custom code or create a new application rather than find a way to make proven tools work. Many projects and careers have died on the "custom solution hill."

Robotic Process Automation (Attended)

Attended RPA is software that complements a person sitting at a workstation, likely using multiple systems and completing rules-based tasks. The "robot" can follow the rules and execute the tasks across systems at high speed and without errors and interact with the human. The attended robot is effectively looking over the work of the agent. While it waits to be called, it prepares potential information and suggested actions based on what the human is doing. Tasks assigned to RPA robotics are generally repetitive, data-entry heavy, rules-based, and fraught with wasted time maneuvering between screens and systems. The term attended applies because the human is involved in the process at points along the way.

Chatbots

Chatbots are simulated people who respond via text on your device. The chatbot allows you to use natural language to ask questions for support and inquires. There are various levels of language recognition. Some are rudimentary. Behind the chat window, a chatbot can execute tasks, access systems, store information for transfer to other systems, and ultimately pass a "chatter" over to a live agent if necessary.

Digital Virtual Assistants

A digital virtual assistant (DVA) is what it sounds like. The easiest examples are Alexa and Siri from Google and Apple, respectively. However, these two examples are only auditory. Advanced virtual assistants go beyond this and include a visual representation of the virtual assistant.

An early and advanced example of this is Amelia, a digital virtual assistant who looks like a racially and age-ambiguous woman. All digital assistants are designed and built to take verbal or written words and respond with answers or actions. In the most advanced implementations, DVAs can handle most customer requirements within a specified scope, like customer service for a mobile phone company.

Workflow Tools

A workflow is a visual diagram of a structured, predefined set of activities that produce a desired result. Workflows can be the basic sequential advancement of steps, or a complex series of events that must parallel with specified dependencies, rules, and requirements. In theory, every time you run the same workflow, you get the same result.

A workflow consists of steps, resources needed to accomplish the steps, and how these interact. Workflows delineate start and end points, the direction(s) of movement, where there may be decision points, what you expect for results, and potential substitute steps. Workflow tools are software programs that help orchestrate the various steps in a process and keep the humans and any assigned robots aligned on what needs to be done next.

Business Process Management

Business process management (BPM) is the methodology and discipline of managing the core processes from the process lens rather than the functional or system lens. BPM focuses on the end-to-end process required to execute an order from start to finish, regardless of the company functions involved and systems used.

There are conflicting views of exactly how this should be done, but many would agree that a full BPM lifecycle includes five core areas: *designing* processes, *modeling* potential results and execution, *execution* of the actual processes, *monitoring* the processes and related systems and data, and finally, *optimizing* the processes for desired outcomes.

Image Recognition And Computer Vision

Computer vision and image recognition are the ability of a computer to recognize something for what it is in human terms. This may sound trivial, but it is quite complicated. The classic examples include showing various pictures of a cat to a computer and trying to get it to define "cat" as a thing. Computer vision combines a wide range of disciplines to interpret visual information and produce a description. This can be a noun, like apple, or a mood, like tired, or a trend, like drying out. A specific for image recognition is facial identification. Image recognition is the input for activities like inventory management and point of sale in stores.

Natural Language Processing

Natural language processing (NLP) is the ability of a computer to listen to or read words spoken naturally by a person and understand what they mean, including tone and mood. Full NLP is the receipt and delivery of natural language. Therefore, NLP also includes generating natural-sounding or written words back to a human who will receive them as they would words spoken or written by a person. NLP does not fully exist in any machine or program; however, rudimentary versions power Siri, Alexa, and the upcoming McDonald's drive-thru windows.

Conversational Artificial Intelligence

The key word is *conversational,* which translates in technology terms to semi-structured, semi-predictable speech that requires interpretation beyond word meanings, grammar, and order to understand. The need is for a machine to understand a human without the human having to speak like a machine. The technology behind this is a complex analysis of actual speech patterns and meaning combined with the machine learning pattern recognition.

Machine Learning

Machine learning is the process of creating algorithms that allow a computer to continuously improve without specific programmed steps to do so but rather by combining experience and data to "learn" to improve outcomes. Commonly misunderstood to be some form of computer magic where the machine becomes some sort of quasi-sentient being, machine learning instead learns from huge data sets and creates patterns to follow from those sets. The algorithms are tested and improved with a separate set of test data.

Though simplistic, if you show enough pictures of a chair, airplane, rotten piece of fruit, or breast tumor to a computer and tell it what it is seeing, then the machine learning algorithm can recognize these going forward. Machine learning platforms are trained in three basic ways:

1. Supervised learning: The machine is shown both the inputs and desired outputs by a human to find recognizable patterns.
2. Unsupervised learning: Data is fed into the machine without labels, and the algorithm uses various analytical tools to find patterns, similarities, categories, and clusters.
3. Reinforcement learning: The computer interacts with a specific environment (e.g., a car or an elevator control system) and works to make adjustments to maximize its reward (e.g., car stays on road, minimum elevator wait time).

Cognitive Computing/Agents

Cognitive computing is the holy grail of artificial intelligence and is meant to do what a human being can do—think or at least simulate thinking. By combing many of the other technologies, including image recognition, NLP, pattern recognition, data mining, and self-learning algorithms, a cognitive computer can begin to behave closer to a human being.

A cognitive computer will be able to take in huge amounts of information and then provide recommendations like medical treatments based on the full patient history and available medical research.

Artificial Intelligence

We have finally reached the umbrella term artificial intelligence. Volumes exist on this, and you need a useful description. General artificial intelligence is the aspiration for a computer to behave in ways that only humans can behave/think. Narrow artificial intelligence is a term that recognizes artificial intelligence capabilities applied within specific boundaries with possible outcomes.

These artificial intelligence capabilities include recognizing objects, patterns, and feelings from words/gestures/tone; understanding natural language; and identifying faces. Narrow artificial intelligence capabilities would also include predicting behavior, identifying trends, seeing order where chaos is obvious, and making recommendations based on all available data that fall within the realm of reasonable and actionable. This is where the money and value of artificial intelligence are today.

One challenge is that over time, what was once something only a human could do is now possible with a computer. For example, what was once impossible, optical character recognition is now routine. The same may well be true for facial recognition, then image recognition, and maybe natural language processing. One writer claimed, "Artificial intelligence is whatever has not been done yet."

Physical Robots

Finally, the technology we all know from the movies. A robot can approach the sophistication of R2D2 or C3PO from *Star Wars* or be as simple as the machines installing windshields in new cars. The addition of the physical element allows the robots to solve more problems and accomplish more tasks than mere software.

An expanded definition of a robot should include self-driving vehicles that are a combination of mechanical and software systems to mimic a human driver. This model could naturally be expanded to include dentists and surgeons.

3 : A FOCUS ON VALUE CREATION

Step Three—Focus on Value Creation

"Act, being well-informed."
The Oracle of Delphi

In the Lao Tzu quote, "The journey of a thousand miles begins with one step," but, you still need to take the first step. In the proverbial journey, the first step, if it is forward, right, or wrong, won't ruin your trip; adjustments can and will be made along the way.

The *Noble Automation Now* Method mostly follows this model. The first step is asking what you are trying to accomplish and how you should do it.

Some cultures lean first toward action. Americans are famous for their propensity to act. Other cultures are more contemplative and take action only after developing a clear plan of approach. Both styles have tradeoffs.

An illustrative example of this phenomenon occurred at the repair facilities of the Yokosuka Naval Base south of Tokyo in the 1980s.

American shipyard executives saw that Japanese shipyard workers were much more productive than their American counterparts stateside. Resisting tribal stereotypes, the executives arranged a test. The lead engineers suspected that simplified explanations such as, "They (Japanese) aren't more efficient; they just work ridiculous hours" were off base. The engineers demanded facts.

The chosen test was the removal and refurbishment of gun mounts on US Navy ships. A five-inch naval gun mount is a large spinning mechanical device that moves the gun, handles ammunition, and penetrates more than twenty feet deep in the deck of a ship. These mounts are complicated, dangerous, and require expertise in mechanics, electronics, hydraulics, and other disciplines to repair. See Figure Five.[27]

The overhaul process for these weapons started when a ship arrived in port for refurbishment. Depending on the gun mount condition, the process could take months, keeping the ships away from their mission of guarding the seas.

Over time, the Navy found the Japanese shipyard workers completed the process approximately 25–30 percent faster. An apples-to-apples test was created to compare an American team and a Japanese team refurbishing the same type of mount.

On day one, the American team jumped on board the ship and got busy disassembling the mount. Meanwhile, the Japanese team went to a conference room, where it spent the next several weeks. Like the proverbial tortoise and the hare, the American hares seemed to be winning over the Japanese tortoises.

Roll forward several months, and the race was over. The Japanese spent the first few weeks planning who was going to do what and in what order. They identified and planned for many complications before stepping aboard the ship. When the contest ended, the Japanese beat the Americans.

Figure 5 Naval Ordnance and Gunnery – NavPers 16116-B - US Government Printing Office, Washington 1952

The story's details are beyond the scope of this book, and I've taken a bit of poetic license, but the point is relevant. As with overhauling naval gun mounts, success with Intelligent Automation means balancing action and a clear plan that tries to predict challenges in advance.

Unlike the gun mount example, many businesses stumble onto automation first as "the next shiny new ball of technology." These new "balls" tend to come along with a wave of hype in the media or someone deep in the organization who loves a particular new technology and wants to play with it. This is not bad if it can be elevated to a business need and executed with a solid plan.

New technology usually lacks use-cases to make it universally obvious how it will help the business. For example, do you think the McDonald's executives saw the first iPad and said, "We can put that in the front of our restaurants and save money while delivering better service"? Unlikely. More realistically, the need to save money and deliver services merged with someone thinking about touchscreens. Innovation was born.

The key is for the business to clearly understand what it needs to improve and then combine that with how it can be done with Intelligent Automation. Planning out the work with Intelligent Automation is analogous to the Japanese shipyard workers planning in the conference room before turning the first wrench.

The most important question is what to work on first. Here are the various ways others have successfully answered that question.

Where To Start

"Why do I rob banks? Because that's where the money is."
Willie Sutton, famous bank robber[28]

We are not robbing banks, but we are setting out to rob the devil of wasted time and human potential. Inspired by Willie Sutton's simplicity, let's go to the opportunities.

Four Promising Places To Start:
- Where you add value for the client
- Where you compare unfavorably to the competition
- Where the actual work is done
- Where your employee epiphanies and innovations lead you

Focusing On Value

A common customer definition of value is a feature, step, or service that the customer is willing to pay you to deliver and will consider when evaluating you against another potential provider. These features include cost, speed, and ease of use. Value also includes the more abstract dimensions like how you made them feel and a sense of professionalism.

Noble Automation should help you directly or indirectly deliver or improve value and provide more of what the customer wants.

You begin by looking at the work. Work steps and functions fall into three groups.

1. **Value-added**: Work done once, something the customer would be willing to pay for, that changes the product or service in some way

2. **Non-value-added**: Something the customer is not willing to pay for, is repeated, and involves no actual change to the product or service

3. **Value-enabling**: Steps required for legal, accounting, or regulatory reasons

Your task with Intelligent Automation should be to eliminate non-value-added steps, speed up value-enabling steps, and improve value-added steps so that the customer directly feels the improved benefit. A methodology for doing this is value stream analysis.

Understanding what your customers see as valuable is as important as finding out what makes your employees feel valued. Some Intelligent Automation changes are made purely to improve the happiness of the employees. These can directly translate to customer satisfaction. This is hard to measure and yet powerful.

You may have to run experiments to determine what your customers think is valuable. For example, it may be profitable to run a machine learning algorithm on the type size, font colors, and backgrounds on your customer-facing webpages to evaluate value-adding dimensions that your customer may not be able to articulate. Costco, for example, runs machine learning algorithms on store placement and movement to maximize revenue.

Do your customers buy more from you or feel better about you when they see Arial type on a blue background with images of aviation or butterflies or some other combination? There are other more complex options beyond your website to explore.

Where The Competition Is Beating You

Intelligent Automation opportunities may come from seeing where you are falling short against the competition. Sources of comparison include customer feedback, market research, or seeking outside advice. The field of industry benchmarking is deep and wide and a fertile ground for comparing yourself to others and finding where you are lacking.

Example: The hotel sends a text message to the customer that says, "Mr. Hodges, we see that you have enjoyed a full breakfast with bacon and eggs on previous stays with us. Would you like us to have that ready for you in the hotel restaurant at 8 a.m.?"

If your hotel does not have that capability and the customer likes it from your competitor, you have a gap to fill.

Gemba: Going To Where The Work Is Done

Gemba is the Japanese word for "where the work is done." Americans might say, "The shop floor." A good way to find the opportunities and challenges is to go to where the work is done. There is no better way to find out what is happening in your company.

Going to the gemba means walking the physical process or storyboarding digital processes from start to finish and identifying what is happening. With digital processes, this means seeing and doing what your customers do and see.

This journey is, almost without exception, a startling experience for anyone in the company. What is happening is usually a mystery because it isn't anybody's job is to understand the whole flow.

Many times, as consultants, we've had to walk the whole process in a company and brief the outcome to the business. On every occasion, someone in the room says, "I did not know we did it that way." Or "I thought we changed the website functionality a long time ago."

When you are looking for opportunities to succeed with Noble Automation, you first can learn how the work is done today.

What Happens When You Don't Tend Your Process Garden

In the words of Phil Kilgore, independent leadership consultant:

"Organizational processes, when unattended, can lead to the largess of the hidden factory, the drop in supplier quality, the rumbling of dissatisfaction in the workforce, sales lagging behind competitors. Just like an aging office worker's health checkup, the best organizations are not asleep at the switch on processes. They don't take their processes or their customers for granted. Are you automating the right pieces of your organization, or any parts of your organizations? Choose the right improvements. Don't dig where you're not likely to find gold!"[29]

Encourage The Innovators

Innovation is sometimes only seen as major breakthroughs like the iPhone or the internet, but millions of smaller innovations change the world for the better.

Innovation can be accomplished in many ways and creating a formula for doing so has always been elusive. However, a few relatively simple steps can increase your team's innovative potential.

Two Types Of Innovators

Michael Kirton, DSc, studied innovation for most of his professional life and gave us a useful innovation framework. His research indicates everyone innovates; we just do it differently. Kirton created a diagnostic instrument to help people learn how they innovate and, more importantly, how they can best work with other people on their teams.

The KAI (Kirton Adaptive Innovative) instrument measures where people fall on a cognitive continuum that presents for our purposes the way they innovate new ideas and improvements.

On one end of the instrument are those he calls *adaptors*—people who make changes within the rules and expectations of the current system, product, or service. You can think of adapters as people who naturally make things better, faster, and cheaper. The adapter tends to turn things up or down or make them wider or narrower to produce a better product or service. While national stereotypes are risky, the Japanese are masters of this form of innovation.

On the other end of the spectrum are what Kirton calls *innovators*. These people tend to come up with ideas that have no clear path back to where they started. These *innovators* may step out of the shower and yell, "I've got it," and come up with a brilliant new idea or a completely laughable failure. Either way, they did not get there following a methodical path of making it bigger, smaller, more rigid, or more flexible. Americans are a natural stereotype for innovators as they generally don't like rules in any form. For more on Kirton's work, see www.kai.foundation.com.

> *"The reason that the American Navy does so well in wartime is that war is chaos, and the Americans practice chaos on a daily basis."*
> **Karl Dönitz, senior Nazi admiral**[30]

This quote can be said of American businesspeople as well. Still, few of us innovate at the end of the spectrum. Rather, we all tend to follow some rules for innovation, and we all have some ideas out of the blue. The key is to figure out how to work with people from the other end and create effective innovations.

Get Input From The Business, Far And Wide

Some of the best ideas for using new technology come from what appear to be epiphanies in the minds of you, your peers, and numerically, most likely, your employees. Actively seeking out ideas from every level of the company has been the secret weapon of the Toyota manufacturing system for decades and many other successful companies outside Japan.

Apple is also famous for its ability to collect, evaluate, and act on innovations throughout the company. If these companies are good examples, then perhaps all epiphanies or ideas should be evaluated for the potential gold they may contain.

During the Tokugawa Shogunate (250 years of unified rule in Japan), the country was not only at peace, but it also achieved much of what we know today to be the mastery of Japanese arts, sword-making, architecture, and culture. This amazing feat was accomplished via an uninterrupted series of rulers called shoguns.[31]

Realizing that all great ideas do not originate with the ruling class, the leader Yoshimune Tokugawa instituted the first recorded use of a suggestion box, which he placed outside the castle walls in 1721. He alone had the key. The ideas were all reviewed, and many were implemented, thereby bypassing the bureaucrats.

Tokugawa understood that everyday people had profound and useful insights and that the traditional hierarchical structure of Japanese society prevented these ideas from making their way to the top of the country.

In Japan, this new openness to epiphanies and suggestions allowed the ruling shogun to make many nationwide improvements in how the government was run. The result was some of the world's most revered mastery in a wide variety of subjects and disciplines.

A similar system is used in Toyota and helped make it the most profitable and best-quality car company in the world. Companies around the world out-compete their rivals with the power of internal suggestions. Roger Krone, CEO of Leidos, has a similar approach to Tokugawa in Japan but no neat box outside his office.[32]

The key to the suggestion box is twofold. First, every idea must be evaluated. Second, the response to every idea must be known. Are these present in your company?

Some new ideas will work brilliantly, and many will fail or not be viable. What you do about that is what matters.

Executive Gold
Brian Duperreault from AIG provided these three golden rules on ideas:
1. The employees know how to help; ask them.
2. Poison for new ideas is taking credit for others' work.
3. Leadership poison is failing to say you are wrong (including your ideas).

The obvious question, assuming you want your company's brilliance, innovation, and epiphanies: How is your (electronic) suggestion box or open door working? Toyota has processed more than 50 million suggestions in fifty-six years. At 350,000 employees, that only makes 2.5 suggestions per employee per year. (I admit they have had greater and fewer employees over the years.)

Geographic Considerations For Noble Automation

Discussing this subject with Laurent Freixe of Nestlé, we talked about how his global firm addressed major technology changes.[33]

Throughout Freixe's tenure at Nestlé, he has identified three types of change.

The Federated Model
The federated model is where each country does what they want and maintains almost complete freedom. This approach maximizes local control and is naturally favored by local leaders. This freedom comes with the cost and difficulty of sharing information with the corporate center and losing centralized spending and coordination potential.

The Centralized Model
In the opposite case, often seen in ERP implementations like SAP or Oracle, the transformation is done from the center of the company, with all the local markets being forced to adapt to the central approach. The benefit of centralized command and control is better visibility but huge upfront costs and coordination. The earlier example where the costly centralized project imploded comes to mind.

The Hybrid Model
The third choice is a hybrid model, where local markets do certain initiatives locally and standardize on other areas. While this sounds more complicated, it can often be the most profitable but requires the most coordination and communication to succeed.

Freixe's final point on geographical implementation was the choice of which markets to go first. He recounted an experience where the company piloted a major change in two medium-sized markets. The benefit of this approach was lowered risk. The cost was a delay in applying the new and better ideas in more sizable and financially important markets.

Good News For Automation
Implementing Intelligent Automaton technology is far less intrusive and risky than implementing a new ERP system. Intelligent Automation technologies are generally additive to the core systems rather than replacements. RPA (robotic process automation), natural language processing, and machine learning technology, for example, interact with the core business systems and can be tried in smaller-scale tests.

Evaluating The Options

At this stage, you will have a healthy list of options to consider from one of the four sources above: where you add value, how you compare to others, what you saw when you walked the work process, and employee innovation epiphanies. The next step is to evaluate and prioritize your options.

Helpful tools here are:

- Balancing the use of technology
- Cost-benefit analysis
- Proof of concept
- Fitting the internal politics

How Much Technology?

In Fremont, California, stands a car factory with a long history of automation and automation disasters. Today the plant is the home to Tesla, and automation has once again become an important and challenging topic there.[34] I will mercifully shorten this story but stick with me—it is illustrative and relevant.

In the 1980s, Japan threatened the American car companies by producing much higher quality cars at low prices. The Fremont plant was owned by General Motors (GM) and was part of a GM plan to catch up with the Japanese car companies.

In what appeared to be an amazing gesture of openness or politically savvy, the Japanese had allowed the US car executives to view their plants via onsite tours. The GM executives had seen the factories of Toyota, Nissan, and Honda and returned to the US with what they thought was the answer—robots.

At that time, the Japanese plants had far more robots than the US plants; so, robots must be the answer, right? This is again the syndrome of the shiny new technology ball. Naturally, the US executives approved plans to outdo the Japanese at their own game. The Fremont plant received a huge investment (billions) to automate and beat the Japanese.[35]

The money was spent, the robots were installed, and the switch was thrown, soon followed by years of disappointment. The GM team could never make the robots work together effectively enough to compete with Toyota, Nissan, and Honda. The Japanese knew this would happen before they opened their doors.

The secret to the Japanese car manufacturing plants was the balance of automation and human action. They called this *autonomation*. In practice, this meant using automation or human action where they made the most sense. Robots would only be put in place when they could outperform humans.

In other words, the Japanese did not automate because it was cool or sexy or on the cover of magazines. They automated because it was the right solution to individual problems and provided unique value along the chain of activity that makes up a complicated business. (Think Luke with a lightsaber and R2D2 with a database—the right tool in the right hands.)

This is the kind of thinking that is working with Intelligent/Noble Automation. The difference is that much of the work is done on PCs rather than on the factory floor. The companies succeeding with the various tools are doing so because they are using them where they make sense and nowhere else. They can do this because their teams do not feel threatened by the technology and open their creative minds to solve the problems.

Cost-Benefit Analysis

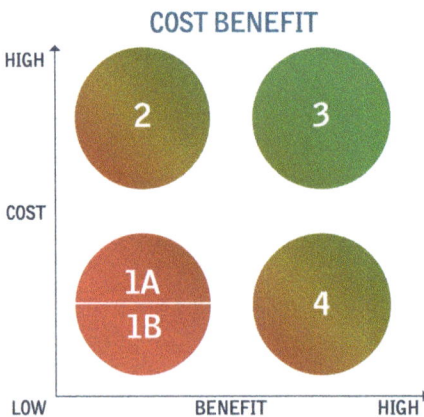

COST BENEFIT

HIGH

COST

LOW   BENEFIT   HIGH

2

3

1A
1B

4

With all that in mind, the matrix below suggests two obvious places to prioritize and one that needs an explanation. This is a simple guide for evaluating automation options. The process starts with asking where you add value and your costs. Visually this can be put in a 2 x 2 matrix. (We consultants do love our 2 x 2 matrices.)

The point is, there are many different business cases for Intelligent Automation, and each will involve different parts of your company. You will benefit from a simple method to track and stack these opportunities.

Cost: This is the measurement of pure financial resources to complete the project, including the salaries and time of the internal team. A harder variable here is to think about opportunity cost, meaning what could these people have done (realistically) if they had not been on this project. This is particularly important when taking frontline salespeople from their pipeline and putting them on projects.

Benefit: These include the financial benefits from the project and subjective benefits. Hard benefits are time savings, reduced errors, and an increase in premium sales uptake by clients. Harder to measure but critically important is employee turnover reduction by making their jobs more enjoyable. It does not take many employees to stay rather than quit to make a project worth the time. The most important benefit of all is perceived customer value improvement.

Quadrant 1: Generally, low-cost and low-benefit projects should be avoided. These are the "who cares" category. If "nobody cares" (1A), these should be avoided as pet projects. However, if someone important in the company who will help future projects succeed cares (1B), then perhaps you should do these projects quickly and leverage the goodwill for more impactful projects.

Quadrant 2: These projects should not be undertaken unless there is a compelling business risk or compliance reason for doing so, like KYC or "Know Your Customer" compliance in financial services.

Quadrant 3: The high-benefit and high-cost projects are attractive but require more thought on the risks and other complications. If your benefits don't materialize and the costs are high, you could poison the well for future projects.

Quadrant 4: Any project with a low cost and high benefit is a "no brainer." If no internal, political, regulatory, or other barrier exists, these should be first.

Proof Of Concept Or Trojan Horse?

The better Noble Automation solutions today begin with a specific business area where improvement will have many supporters. A scope of work is then designed to use the minimum new technology to achieve the biggest overall improvement, often called a proof of concept (POC).

A POC should be what it says—proof that your idea will work on a small scale and be done quickly enough to maintain enthusiasm and excitement. When POCs work, this is exactly what they do.

However, a POC can often be a way for a consulting or technology company to sell you their solution (the Trojan Horse) rather than the solution that may be in your best interest overall. This is usually not done malevolently but rather because of their familiarity with a limited range of tools or approaches.

Mea Culpa

As a consulting partner in a major firm, I successfully sold a large consulting project to a telecom client in Sweden. The success made me feel like a hero and then a goat. The software solution I sold the client and the implementation to make it work was a wonderful answer to their needs if you didn't consider the other software available to solve the problem better.

After months of negotiations and presentations and internal selling by the client teams, we won, and the contract was signed. The client got what they paid for, but it was not what they could have had if I been smarter about other options.

Many months later, I was asked to speak at an industry conference by a company that had a better solution for that client. Their solution would have raised my telecom client's game and improved their key metrics if I had only known it existed.

Moral of the story: The risk in working with outside help is that they may know quite a bit about some solutions and be blind to others. In the words of former US President Ronald Reagan, "You should trust but verify" that they are helping you see a wide enough range of options.[36]

Warlords Or Leadership Team?

Another key point to consider is evaluating the business leaders in the areas you may want to automate. Specifically, this is where understanding office power and politics is so important.

Golden Tip

Some HR leaders are truly business partners with deep insights to the people who run your company. These professionals can be essential in helping you navigate these waters. If your HR leadership does not have the necessary gravitas and insight, then perhaps find another executive sage with whom you can collaborate.

Great projects and automation ideas can be killed by Machiavellian antics in the executive suite. You are not going to use Noble Automation to fix the politics and power struggles in any company, so the best advice is to understand the motivations and behaviors of the players and make that part of your planning on what to do first and who to involve. Find a win-win if possible. If you are the CEO, this problem is much simpler but still not zero.

Act Like A Team Of Good Doctors

In the best hospitals, doctors work in patient-centered teams. Each specialist has his/her focus area and their shared medical school education, but we patients are complicated machines indeed.

For much of medical history, patients either had one doctor who tried to be all things (early days of medicine) or a series of specialist doctors. Though doctors would wince at this analogy, having only a specialist see you is a bit like having a carpenter with only a hammer build your house. Yes, the carpenter knows other tools have value, but if they only have a hammer— ; you know where this goes.

Doctors empirically get better patient results when they can collaborate with other specialists to holistically treat the patient. They still have disagreements on protocol, but these at least see the light of day when the doctors speak to each other.[37]

Businesses are similar when looking for Noble Automation opportunities. Better results come when people who understand their specific pieces collaborate with those who understand other pieces. This requires culture and incentives that support collaboration.

Zen And The Art Of Noble Automation

With your prioritized list of opportunities in hand, cost-benefit completed, a good handle on your technology appetite, and your plan adjusted for how your leaders work, it's time to take a deep breath and maybe add a little Zen thinking.

The book *Zen and the Art of Motorcycle Maintenance* by Robert Pirsig does not mention automation, but it does speak poignantly to two categories of thinkers who both play a role in success with Noble Automation.

One category of person can be described as the romantic thinker who sees the world as a series of gestalts or just "being in the moment." The other category is the classic rational thinker who revels in understanding how things work and the joys of keeping them working—motorcycles in the book's example.[38]

As a teenager, many of the deeper philosophical points were over my head. However, one story stuck in my mind and relates directly to Noble Automation.

In the book, four people travel across the country on two motorcycles. One bike is driven by a husband and wife, both romantics. The other is driven by the narrator, a classical thinker, with his son as a passenger.

The romantics have chosen to buy an expensive BMW bike, and the narrator is riding an older, less expensive machine.

The BMW, at some point, has a mechanical problem. The mechanic in a small town tells the romantic owner that his expensive German machine needs a part that will take many days to secure. The delay would effectively end their trip. The narrator, a classic thinker, maintains his motorcycle and suggests that a flat piece of a soda can, cut just so, will suffice for the expensive part and keep them on the road.

A schism develops between the romantic, who bought a BMW to shield him from thinking about how things work, and the classical thinker, who sees the journey as the important goal and knowing how the bike works as an integral and joyful part getting there.

The point for Intelligent Automation is to have a vision for the business and align your classical and romantic thinking. If having your technology perfectly integrated and seamlessly running your business like the gears of a BMW or Swiss watch is more important than serving your clients and paying your employees, you may find yourself metaphorically stopped in a gas station in Montana waiting for a part. In business, this would be stopped waiting for perfection while the competition passes you by.

During the Cold War, both the Russians and the Americans built intercontinental ballistic missiles. These are precise and complicated weapons. The singular point of the missile is to get to the target and detonate.

Engineers from both countries struggled with balancing the weight distribution of the missiles so they would fly straight. The American engineers meticulously arranged the parts and precisely machined the missile cones to be balanced. The Russians spun their imbalanced missiles on a table and added weights inside the cone like a tire mechanic does on an automobile. Both approaches worked, but the Americans spent more money.

A timely example came from a conversation with the global leadership development executive of a top-three investment bank. She shared how COVID had forced their bank to abandon rigid protocols for working, communicating, and making decisions. If they had not flexed and relaxed some processes, the bank would cease to function.

This is exactly the Zen metaphor from above. COVID forced the bank's rigid thinking and buttoned-up shirts to relax on non-essential steps and processes. Their version of the soda can cut just so was decision-making done informally via DocuSign (online signature software) and allowing sensitive work to be done from home.

In practical terms, Zen and the art of Noble Automation means focusing on the journey (business success) while introducing your company to as much romantic thinking, design elegance, and intuitive execution as possible. It's okay to use workarounds, Band-Aids, duct tape, and spreadsheets where necessary, so long as the journey and progress continue.

Summary: *Noble Automation Now* Method Step Three

- Succeeding with Noble Automation is like Lao Tzu's journey of one thousand miles—it begins with a first step and a place to start.

- Focusing on where you add value in your business is likely a rich vein to mine.

- Using Intelligent Automation to fill gaps in the performance of your current business or to match your competition is likely to inspire and motivate your team.

- Balancing your use of technology and keeping from the extremes of too little or too much is essential.

- Though Noble Automation is a detailed and methodical application of technologies, many great implementation ideas come from morning shower-like epiphanies to which the wise and lucky give an audience.

- All efforts must be reviewed in the cold light of cost-benefit tradeoffs tempered by the realism of political receptivity.

- Blending the romantic and rational thinkers was the goal in *Zen and the Art of Motorcycle Maintenance*; perhaps it should also be the goal of Zen and the art of Noble Automation.

4 : EMPOWERED & EXCITED TEAMS

Step Four—Empowered and Excited Teams

"I don't know what people think I do all day,
but I spend 95 percent of my time on people."
Alan Colberg, CEO, Assurant[39]

The next step in the Noble Automation Now Method is to excite and empower your people.

Maybe you remember the epiphany that people were the hard part while technology, processes, and numbers were more straightforward. Maybe you had this epiphany early in your career or yesterday. The latter is just in time, because succeeding with Noble Automation is mostly about the people.

Can you transform your current business, change fundamental processes, master new technologies, and achieve your numbers with less than half your current team? Probably not, yet for many businesses, this is the challenge. The cause is a lack of employee engagement. According to Gallup, only 36 percent of employees are actively engaged with their jobs and companies.[40]

Assuming your strategy is sound, the number one cause of success or failure is employee engagement, ultimately driving execution. If your employees are excited about their jobs, interested in what your company does, and see a future for themselves, everyone wins. If too few feel this way, you will likely fail tomorrow or soon. Those are the hard facts, which, in your gut, you already know because you have been that junior employee. Feels like yesterday, doesn't it?

Those Darn Millennials

The frequent refrain is millennial/young employees are entitled or overly demanding or self-centered/absorbed and too hard to motivate. This is mostly a baby boomer or Gen-X misconception and misses the key point. Granted, some employees take themselves too seriously and are too self-absorbed to see the company succeed. Perhaps the bigger issue is that these talented young people ask what their parents' generation would have asked for if they thought they could have it.

For example, do you think your peers would have demanded bosses who paid attention to them, allowed them room to grow, and put deep thought into their development? As a baby boomer, I know the bosses I had who did show genuine interest received my full attention and loyalty. I also know my bosses who didn't show genuine interest in my success received less acclaim and often disdain.

Good leaders, from the Roman legions to today's tech companies, pay attention to their troops and receive in return loyalty, energy, hard work, and yes, engagement.

How big a problem is this for your company?

1. Are most employees giving most of their effort to the job and your company?
2. Do you think this is a key driver to your company's success?
3. Does your leaders' talk match their walk on employee engagement?

Here is a quote from the most respected CEO of the twentieth century, who I worked for, and the former editor of the *Harvard Business Review*:

"No company, small or large, can win over the long run without energized employees who believe in the firm's mission and understand how to achieve it. That's why you need to take the measure of employee engagement at least once a year through anonymous surveys in which people feel completely safe to speak their minds."
Jack and Suzy Welch[41]

Gallup, the international analytics and advisory company, is a leader in polling, research, and specifically studying employee engagement. Their research across countries and companies, polling thousands of people, measures three categories of employee sentiment. They support the broader research identifying engagement as a critical success factor. They describe employee sentiment in three categories:[42]

Engaged	Highly involved, enthusiastic, and committed to their work and the company
Not engaged	Just doing their job, putting in time
Actively disengaged	Miserable in their job, spreading discontent among their peers

Let's look at some concrete examples of the various engaged types.

The Engaged Employee

An engaged employee usually comes to work in a good mood. They look for opportunities to delight customers and colleagues or make the company better. They work toward solutions as opposed to standing around complaining. Their resumé is probably not up-to-date, they don't discreetly carry a personal phone and a work phone, and they are seen occasionally with company-branded merchandise. They talk freely about their company to friends and maybe on social media.

Engaged people recommend their company to others. They don't drive Fords onto the Toyota employee lot or vice versa, and they don't sleep under their desks (yes, a real observed example). The engaged employees are your stars to collect and allow to shine.

The Actively Disengaged Employee

This employee frequently complains about the company, boss, products, lunchroom, etc. They reluctantly admit where they work in social encounters. They don't own a company polo shirt, and they sure as hell would not recommend anyone they know to apply to work here.

Most importantly for our topic, the actively disengaged employee reluctantly joins teams and then as virtual prisoners. They delay projects and find reasons that ideas will fail. These are the proverbial organization "buzz killers." They should be invited to find their fortune elsewhere.

A rare and tragic example of good employee disengagement was the manufacturing workers of Oskar Schindler in World War II mentioned previously.

The Not-Engaged Employee

This is the toughest and sadly largest category of employees. The not-engaged employee doesn't necessarily do anything wrong but rarely goes beyond the minimum expectation. You can't quite put your finger on whether the person isn't bright or doesn't care. No stimuli seem to work and when 5 p.m. rolls around, this person is gone or offline (COVID world). The good news is that these folks can be brought into the engaged category through good leadership, but they are often not.

> *"I don't worry about the top 20 percent; they are motivated and making things happen. I worry about the middle 50 percent who are not giving us all they have to give."*
> **CHRO, global toy company**

For our purposes, key points and benefits from Gallup's research[43] on employee engagement include:

- Employee engagement is essential to successful competition and profitability.
- Engaged employees treat customers better and attract new ones.
- Engaged employees are more likely to stay in the company.
- What drives employee engagement includes tangible motivations (benefits) and intangible motivations (opportunities to develop).
- Good leadership and development opportunities are the biggest factors driving engagement today.
- After a January 2020 high, employee engagement has fallen dramatically.
- In early 2021, about 36 percent of employees were engaged, 14 percent were actively disengaged, and the remaining 50 percent were just putting in the time.

Where To Start With Employee Engagement

Clearly, as we embark on putting Noble Automation to work, we need more fully engaged employees. If Gallup is correct, our problems transcend automation.

Two essential questions to gauge your employee engagement challenges:

1. What can you do to engage more employees who are currently not engaged?
2. Will you act on the actively disengaged employees?

Let's start with what is keeping people from being engaged in the first place.

The Outliers And Misfits

Some employees are simply miserable in their lives, in the wrong company, job, country, marriage, whatever, meaning they are unhappy people who may need a therapist more than a good manager, and you're likely not a therapist. Mental health is a serious subject and one most of us managers are not equipped to handle professionally.

Mental health aside, these are not the people we can help. This sounds harsh, but it is also true. The amount of resources dedicated to moving an actively disengaged person to engaged is huge and takes away from your better and more motivated employees. It may be your company's fault that they feel this way, or it may be something else; by the time people get to this point, it doesn't matter. Elvis (i.e., their commitment) has left the building.

On the positive side, we can help the actively disengaged and the company by quickly identifying these folks and compassionately exiting them from the company as soon as possible. The sooner they leave, the sooner they can find a place where they are actively engaged. Fortunately, these folks are few, but like arsenic, a small amount can kill the patient or company.

At the end of the next step is advice from several senior leaders of Fortune 500 businesses on treating people with compassion, especially when the direction is exiting them from the business.

*"Whenever our company must reduce our employee base,
which keeps me up at night, I start with the toxic few,
the cancer to our company. Knowing these people are
first helps me make more difficult decisions regarding
good people trying to do their jobs."*
CHRO, global toy company

Engagement Equals Meaning, Health, And Purpose

With the difficult category behind us, what about the far more important group of people who would love to be inspired but are not? This is where we can make magic for the company and our colleagues' lives.

We can start with a quote from retired Cambridge University Professor Dame Carol Black:

*"For most people, their work is a key determinant of self-worth,
family esteem, identity, and standing within the community,
besides of course material progress and a means of
social participation and fulfillment."*[44]

In other words, work is incredibly important to a person's life and health; therefore, we have every reason to help our employees become actively engaged in their jobs and our companies. So, what is employee engagement, and what brings it up?

Understanding What Drives Employee Engagement

Employee engagement is the harnessing of people's identity to their work roles; when engaged, people employ and express themselves physically, cognitively, and emotionally during role performances. Further, since humans are different, engagement is better measured against an individual's potential rather than some universal scale.[45]

Seven generally recognized key elements drive employee engagement and many peripheral dimensions, like great food in the company cafeteria.

Let's focus on the big seven:[46]
- Integrity, purpose, and values of the company
- Knowing what is expected of me, what is success
- Believing my job is important
- Frequency, value, and content of internal communications
- Potential to grow and be promoted
- Satisfying working relationships
- Availability of constructive feedback

Integrity, purpose, and values of the company. People want to work somewhere that passes their friends' dinner or pub test question: "So what is your company like?" Specifically, most people want to work somewhere that becomes an extension of their aspirations to be a good, meaningful, and valuable person.

Bad example: The owner of a small consulting company was driving in a rental car with three subordinates when he realized that the fuel gauge was not working. Laughing, he said: "We can drive it till it's empty and then turn it in without having to fill up the tank, just like I did in Dallas."

In one sentence, he declared, "We will steal resources from our providers and screw over the next driver who thinks the car is full." Think what that says about his ethics. Not surprisingly, this real-life business owner was later in a series of lawsuits and sued by several business partners for breach of contract. He was last seen looking into politics.

Good example: Roger Krone, CEO of Leidos, works in a highly secure and sensitive industry. Leidos helps manage electronic health records for active-duty service members. Protecting personal information and national secrets is a core value of the company. On the rare occasion that someone irreparably breaks that trust, the company can't continue to employ them.[47]

Tolerating violations of integrity is not acceptable. Still, Krone recognizes the humanity of the situation, and if there isn't a good fit with the company's values and culture, he does everything he can to ensure they can leave the company with their pride intact.

*"How you exit people matters, and it matters a lot.
These good, well-meaning people just don't fit into the team.
Treat them with dignity and respect and they can become ambassadors
for your company within your industry community when they depart."*
Roger Krone, CEO, Leidos

Knowing what is expected of me and what success is. Essential to feeling professional satisfaction is knowing what your organization defines as success. Rare is the actively engaged person who does not know how success is measured for their role. Ambiguous success criteria leads to anxiety and disengagement.

> **Bad example:** Examples of this are endemic to big companies. A common example is when a manager says to a subordinate, "Put together a report on this situation and send it to me by Friday. By the way, I will be unavailable for the rest of the week to discuss it."

> The employee then struggles to figure out exactly what is expected of him/her and likely spends far too much time creating something the manager may not even want.

> Fear of disappointing the manager then fills his/her mind. Adding insult to injury, many managers then don't value the output they get nor give clear guidance for the next report.

> **Good example:** Linda Passarelli, vice president of Talent Management at Fidelity Canada, shared a story about why she is so adamant about clear expectations with employees.[48]

> A long-term employee was not meeting internal client expectations. The problem was in the employee's approach, not her knowledge or experience. The employee was in the wrong job. After fretting too long over the situation, Passarelli moved the person to another role where she later thrived, but Passarelli hadn't discussed the core problem.

> Only later, when the dust settled, and much unnecessary employee anxiety had passed, did Passarelli realize clearer expectations and a definition of success would have made the move a win for all. Lesson learned.

As a result of this early hiccup, Passarelli makes setting clear expectations a major training focus with her whole organization.

Believing my job is important. Employee engagement is directly correlated with how important others perceive their role. Companies with respected and marginalized roles see a matching bifurcation in employee engagement.

> **Bad example:** How often have you heard someone say disparagingly, "Oh, he is (only) in operations or finance or IT" or any function other than the big deal winner? This message is as insidious as "you are our dumb or worthless child," yet it happens all the time.

> This phenomenon occurs because of a tiered respect culture perpetuated by poor or oblivious leaders. The signs may be subtle, but employees are good at reading the tea leaves when they or their functions are not valued.

> **Good example:** Pre-COVID, I attended an all-employee company event arranged on the island of Sardinia, which required an enormous amount of coordination, logistics, and planning for the five hundred people. One speaker gave a compelling talk on the power of relationships that required his preparation and months of video interviews and careful editing by a team.

> Before wrapping up and before the audience could applaud for his stage performance, the speaker asked the team who'd made his speech content possible to join him on stage for the well-deserved recognition. Teams get great things done and recognizing them begets more great things.

Frequency, value, and content of internal communications. Humans are largely social creatures, some highly so but all to some degree. Communications that are accurate, timely, and valuable are the lubricant making the human machine turn smoothly.

> **Bad example:** I once worked in an office where layoffs were frequent as the economy sputtered. Leadership did not explain to the business what was happening or why. Instead, cardboard boxes would show up in the hallways on Friday when layoffs would happen on Monday. When

we saw the boxes, we all knew what was happening and assumed the worst, repeatedly. That CEO was also known for the scotch on his breath at noon. Correlation or causation?

Good example: When COVID hit Mercer, a global consulting company, the firm was pushed hard like the whole industry. Everyone knew the challenges would be big, and anxiety quickly rose to a fever pitch. Fortunately, the leadership team, according to Anita Lefebvre, chief people officer of Operations and Technology, were over-achievers by being exceptional and prolific communicators.[49]

Through regular pulse surveys, active individual outreach, open forums where people shared their concerns, and most importantly, with crystal clear information on the company's plans, people remained calm and committed. Well done, Mercer.

Potential to grow and be promoted. Not all people seek advancement, but nearly all seek growth. Those who don't seek advancement or growth are rarely engaged with the natural advance of progress and activity in the company. Engaged people want to grow and get promoted to the level where they feel rewarded and valued.

Bad example: "You can't get promoted here until you have been a _____ for two years." This is a clear statement that it isn't worth bringing your full brain to the game because you can't break the promotion timeline.

Making it worse, the employee often does not know what it takes to get promoted and goes on a blind search for the formula, which often turns out to include far too much politics.

Good example: Eric Kirsch, CIO of Aflac, recounted a pattern where some employees' expectations for pay or promotion did not align with how the executive team valued the person's contributions.

In response, Kirsch made it clear to his team that it was their job to make sure people knew what was expected of them. He further set the expectation that his subordinate managers would help employees find the opportunities they needed to prove themselves. Success on the projects was, of course, up to the employee.

This combination of clarity and opportunity gave the employees a clear target and increased their engagement and contributions.[50]

Availability of constructive feedback. Perhaps most important to employee engagement is direct performance and behavior feedback. All companies provide feedback, much of which is primitive, clumsy, or sporadic. Clear, timely, and constructive feedback is the rare, free, and immensely powerful driver of engagement.

Bad example: Annual feedback that is out-of-date and non-specific does not help. Worse yet, the boss says, "Hey, could you write up a summary of what you did this year so we can talk about it?" These managers, in my opinion, should be reeducated or removed. Less drastic would be having the person who provides the feedback be the person who knows what the employee did.

As an officer in the navy, I was asked to document what I did and write my fitness report (evaluation) word for word. This still happens today. Just how genuine does it feel when you must write what a wonderful job you did? The best navy leaders do not do this, and there are many.

Good example: The manager calls the subordinate into their office and says something like this: "Ashley, according to my records, you worked on project A and project B recently, and you did the following well, and the following had challenges. How did this go for you? What did you think? How can I help you? By the way, your next assignments include this and that, and they should stretch you. Good luck, and I am always here to help."

In thirty years of work, seeing leaders who genuinely care is as rare as Harry Potter's sorcerer's stone and just as powerful. Jack Welch was one of these people, and so are US Navy Commander Anne McKinney, Captain David Santucci, and former GE executives Richard Gumbrecht and Terry Sheehan, to name a few.

Satisfying working relationships. Employees want to get along with their fellow employees, work with their customers, and find satisfaction and professional harmony with their boss. People generally quit bosses, not companies, and engaged employees connect with their boss, colleagues, and customers in that order.

Bad example: This is the boss everyone talks about behind their back because he/she is one or more of these: a coward, self-serving egotist, showboat who steals credit for others' work, liar, corporate politician, or snake. Worst among these traits is the boss unwilling to give credit where it belongs and takes it themselves.

I once accepted a position working for a person I had not yet met. Big mistake. I later learned his international reputation was that of managing up and dumping down. I also once worked for a man known internally for womanizing with junior employees and selling lots of work.

Fortunately, these are exceptions, and I have worked with more admirable and wonderful people than these, but some you just never forget.

Good example: I was once part of a team of eight project managers, all working on projects to improve our business unit. While we didn't all love every project we were doing, we did love the harmony and support from the team. We shared ideas, contributed to other's projects, collaborated on shared solutions, and created real value for the business.

As a team, we also went to dinner together, celebrated, and connected, willingly, occasionally outside the office. As a result, most of us stayed in our roles longer than we would have had it not been for the team. People really do tend to quit bosses, not companies.

Gallup uses a twelve-question survey to poll employees on how they are feeling about their work you may find helpful.[51]

Gallup Twelve Elements Of Employee Engagement Questions

1. I know what is expected of me at work.
2. I have the materials and equipment I need to do my work right.
3. At work, I can do what I do best every day.
4. In the last seven days, I have received recognition or praise for doing good work.
5. My supervisor, or someone at work, seems to care about me as a person.
6. There is someone at work who encourages my development.
7. At work, my opinions seem to count.
8. The mission or purpose of my organization makes me feel my job is important.

9. My associates or fellow employees are committed to doing quality work.
10. I have a best friend at work.
11. In the last six months, someone at work has talked to me about my progress.
12. This last year, I have had opportunities at work to learn and grow.

Employee Engagement Implications For Successful Noble Automation

So, what does this mean for Noble Automation specifically? It is quite easy to get overwhelmed with the research and data and simply become paralyzed about what to do next. You are a businessperson and not a researcher, so let's focus on the practical.

There are short-run actions many of us can take. The best place to start is to assess your organization now and work on the weak spots directly connected to automation/artificial intelligence.

Remember the situation:

- Many people are in routine, boring jobs and likely to be replaceable by some form of automation. Data entry, swivel chair computing, and monotonous work are all on the way out.
- Many people are doing work that directly goes against what humans do best—think, feel, interact, and solve problems.
- Mistakes from people doing boring work consume valuable time and crush morale.
- Many on your team are eager to help make the business better; they want to be engaged, not wasting time on expense reports or navigating disconnected systems.
- Many lower and mid-level employees on your team worry about losing their jobs.

Suggested Actions

Knowing what *not to* do may be helpful. In many business transformation cases, jobs will be lost. Too often, the manager says to his team something like this:

"Thank you all for being on the team to improve the business. We expect this new project to change the way we work and save us money. We ask you ten people to create a better process that only requires six of you."

As absurd as this sounds, this is frequent and common in many countries. Putting yourself in the shoes of the people on this team would help avoid this. Unfortunately, managers are often most focused on getting the project done.

The worst outcome from scenarios like above is that the best employees get nervous, and like the best swimmers in a sinking ship, they jump overboard. The average employees partly shut down and start looking for internal options to protect their jobs. The worst employees add even less value and are often dazed and confused by the changes. No wonder 70 percent of transformations fail.

As you move forward with Noble Automation and develop your plan around business areas and technologies, your employees will fall into three categories:

1. **Upwardly mobile:** These employees' roles will change from automation and some will be promoted.
2. **Augmented workers:** These employees' roles will remain largely the same.
3. **No longer fit:** These employees will leave and hopefully find success elsewhere.

As you develop the overall transformation plan, a people strategy for each category will make the entire process more likely to succeed. Human resources is critical. Again, from personal experience, I have seen a wide variety of ways that leadership views and works with HR leaders.

If your company's history does not include genuinely valuing HR, you may not have hired, retained, and developed HR professionals to be business partners; you may look to the HR bench and be disappointed. However, many HR professionals are eager to be business partners and will rise to the occasion when the executives tap them on the shoulder to help. Reminiscent of Humphrey Bogart in *Casablanca*, "This could be the beginning of a beautiful relationship."

Jack Welch, GE CEO, would visit businesses and attend meetings and conferences with his CHRO Bill Conaty and not his CFO or sales leaders. Bill was Jack's trusted business partner and always scanning for talent to develop. This is a best practice for leaders like you today or in the future. When I reached out to Bill for this book, I found he is out there still supercharging businesses with advice on developing leaders.

A Note on HR Professionals

Some organizations deeply value their HR team and consider them business partners. These organizations have a good chance of succeeding with Noble Automation.

Other organizations act as if HR is unimportant. These organizations will likely struggle with Noble Automation.

Action: If you don't value your HR team as business partners, consider fixing this, one way or the other.

Developing A People Plan For Noble Automation

Turning to the positive, if your organization has a developed method for evaluating and developing people in project work like Noble Automation, then you are off to the races and at least one step ahead. If your organization does not have this approach nailed down, here is a framework that may help. It is called HEPAC.

The point of HEPAC is to make the changes that will benefit the business while being proactive about the workforce and keeping your best employees on board and motivated.

Here is the model:

Humanize	Start with remembering these are human beings just like you and commit to treating them like you want to be treated.
Evaluate	Evaluate your team for the needed skills, their ability to learn, and their personal career goal fit with a business focused on Intelligent Automation.
Plan	Create an individual plan for all those involved and impacted to include job changes, promotions, and exits.
Act	Inform each employee where they stand and what you have to offer them in the future.
Communicate	Communicate to the business what is taking place and what it means for the future, specifically their personal future.

Success Accelerator

If done diligently and with the respect that your team deserves, they will remain almost completely focused on the project at hand and working toward a successful outcome. They will do this because they know they are developing as people, and that is a huge driver for employee engagement.[52]

- For those staying in the company in new roles, the Noble Automation project will be a badge of achievement.

- For those staying in the company and working with the new technology, the project will build skills and upgrade their work quality.

- For those involved but who ultimately leave the company, the experience will be a solid resume bullet.

If managed professionally, everyone will either win or be treated with respect and move on in their career.

The above frameworks and questions are high-level guides. Effective execution will require ironing out the details for your organization and applying best practices for feedback, planning, and compassionate treatment of your team.

Doing this "hard stuff" will require business leaders, HR professionals, and executives to work as a team. Your goal, if you wish to accept it, is to financially succeed and "help humans be heroes." That is the subject of the next chapter.

Summary: Noble Automation Now Method Step Four

- Achieving Noble Automation or any other profound change in your business is all about the people.

- Employee engagement is the current way to describe people being focused on making your business succeed.

- Employee engagement is the primary responsibility of leaders.

- Employees are engaged, not engaged or actively disengaged. There are proven approaches for working with each category.

- Employee engagement can be raised dramatically by paying genuine attention to people. There are seven keys and metrics:
  - Integrity, purpose, and values of the company
  - Knowing what is expected of me, what is success
  - Believing my job is important
  - Frequency, value, and content of internal communications
  - Potential to grow and be promoted
  - Satisfying working relationships
  - Availability of constructive feedback

- The HEPAC method is a reliable tool to keep your best employees on board.

- Some employees cannot be helped and need to be shown a dignified exit.

- HR leaders can be a huge advantage to business leaders in making and succeeding with strategic change.

Step Five: Helping Humans Be Heroes

*"Few among us have realized our full potential.
Moving toward that potential, is the highest cause.
Helping others do so is noble leadership and the path to loyalty."*
Commander Thomas Shine Jr., US Navy[53]

The next step in the Noble Automation Now Method is to create leadership that will help humans be heroes.

Speaking of heroes, the earlier mentioned characters in *Star Wars* are a metaphor for how humans and automation can work together well. In the first film, Luke starts in his dull backwater planet, receives a call to adventure, conquers great evil, and saves the galaxy.

Most importantly, this pattern repeats not just in movies but in life. It is called the hero's journey.

Star Wars was a fun movie series to watch, but what does it have to do with real life? In a city, town, or at the other end of a Zoom call right now, millions of people, old and young, face the challenge of living with endless drudgery and repetition.

They each have untapped human potential and are in varying degrees aware they are in a rut. They are heroes such as Luke, Leia, Han Solo, Harry Potter, and Dorothy from the *Wizard of Oz*. Like you, they long for adventure, achievement, and meaning at a level beyond what they have today.

Many wish they could leave their "planet" (your company?), even if that only means another town or changing jobs to something less mundane. Many others are simply terrified that they may lose their only job, a psychological proxy to death.

Meanwhile, out beyond their sight are leaders and managers who can see the threat of impending change coming from a menacing force called artificial intelligence and the Fourth Industrial Revolution. Just as in *Star Wars*, some enthusiastically say this revolution will bring "order" to the universe (profit, growth, and bonuses), while millions more see the change as a tangible threat to their very existence.

Supporting this fear, many have seen not their farms burned like Luke, but their friends or family laid off as some technology comes to replace them. Some find themselves standing in line at the local McDonald's, ordering food on the touchscreen display, and wondering when the threat of technology will reach their doorstep and stop their paycheck. Others just wonder when automation will climb the food chain to their job.

Rather than the walls of the Death Star trash compactor closing in, the drumbeat of technology hype slowly quickens as the press and Hollywood increasingly paint the impending changes as revolutionary and all-encompassing. Even more outlandish numbers of jobs are labeled "at-risk," and the fear-mongers do what fear-mongers do, predict doom.

In *Star Wars*, Luke and his friends have gambled so much and have such high hopes to be part of a greater future, yet there they sit, stuck in the muck.

In our world, we find ourselves somewhat like Luke and company. Our hearts are captivated by the dream of meaningful work, careers, and ever-improving lives for ourselves and those we love. Yet today, more than ever, many feel prevented from achieving this. Instead, they are metaphorically stuck in the trash compactor of doom, fearing the demon of artificial intelligence.

At the same time, we leaders and executives see this sparkling new tool that may help us achieve our goals and compete in the relentless global business world. This is a paradox that has many paralyzed, frustrated, and looking for answers.

This book aims to help leaders and individuals see a hero's journey for every person—to help them find great purpose in what they are doing, push themselves to new levels, and in the process, make companies dramatically more successful and profitable.

What Is A Hero?

A hero or heroine is a person who, in the face of danger, overcomes adversity through feats of ingenuity, bravery, or strength. A hero is a person who realizes more of their potential than the average or normal person and achieves some inspirational goal, including conquering their lesser selves.

So why do we need heroes at work? After all, in our companies, we are not saving the universe or winning a world war or championing civil rights in our time. Most of us are working in businesses that are small parts of a larger economy. How do we get inspired, or more importantly, inspire others?

Introducing Joseph Campbell

Joseph Campbell was the leading authority on myths and mythology worldwide up to his death in 1987. His book, *Hero of a Thousand Faces,* is a fascinating read on mythology, but more importantly, his perspective on how we can learn from myths and see them in our own lives. This may be one of the most important subjects you ever read about as a leader and person.[54]

Campbell studied myths and stories from cultures as varied as the Aztecs to the Japanese, Inuit, Russians, and his favorite, Native American tribes of North America. He found that most of the lasting stories, regardless of origin, followed a pattern he later called the hero's journey. You will recognize the hero's journey at the very least in the *Star Wars*-inspired segment written above, but that is one of thousands of like tales.

Campbell's work is the touchstone for this idea of mythology in daily lives. The film *Finding Joe*[55] does a marvelous job of making these ideas more visual. For our purposes, let me summarize the hero's journey as three major phases.

RETURN · SEPARATION · THE HERO'S JOURNEY · INITIATION

Separation is where the potential hero is inspired to break away from the routine, standard, low-risk, hometown way of doing things. The separation is from the comfortable and limiting.

When the hero becomes aware of the limiting aspects of his/her life, he/she is primed and ready to hear the "call to adventure," which quickly leads to initiation.

Initiation is where the hero has made the clear break from the past and is now to be educated and indoctrinated to the ways of the better state. There are many trials and tribulations in this phase that eventually end up in the darkest of caves, facing the strongest of dragons. Only when our hero learns to face these dragons does providence move to help him/her.

Some event or combination of events become the crossing of a threshold. Doors then open only for our hero and opportunity presents itself that would otherwise have been elusive. This takes us to the final phase, the return.

Return is when the hero, having overcome many challenges and conquered his/her dragon, has accomplished the mission and then returns to his/her former land a changed person. Only then does the hero share the spoils of victory with former countrymen, in some cases only knowledge.

Generals and Dragons

One of my hero journeys was working at General Electric. Our team worked eighteen months on a difficult project. We received the needed wise advice, overcame dragons, fought internal bureaucracy, and finished with tough deadlines.

Our "return" was the opportunity to present to GE Chairman Jack Welch. He did, as Campbell would say all great leaders do, let us shine and received reflected glory in the process.

Only years later did I see this as a hero's journey. By then, I was fighting my next dragon in Japan.

This cycle repeats, like the *Star Wars* series, until we individually run out of time on the planet.

Humans, like movie characters, are not happy when they sit like the Hobbit Bilbo Baggins in the shire, becoming full, dumb, and happy. We get restless in spirit and body. As with Bilbo, we have often forgotten the last call to adventure and tell ourselves a peaceful life is best. We resist the next call, but eventually, like Campbell's metaphorical phone, it will keep ringing until we pick it up and begin our next adventure.

The alternative, all too common in real life, is to ignore the call by numbing ourselves with food, drugs, alcohol, or social media.

To complicate things, the next call to adventure arrives in a different form than the previous iteration. Maybe you get fired or divorced, or COVID 20XX changes the course of your career; but make no mistake, the cycle repeats, and now you have a new dragon.

This dragon may be larger or smaller than the first. This dragon may require improving your own life or those of others. All you know for sure is that it is your next dragon.

This pattern, according to Campbell, is the pattern not just for myth but for our lives, because it is from real lives that our human predecessors have drawn the core principles for our myths. We are Luke and Rei Skywalker, Harry Potter, Hermione Granger, Indiana Jones, and many other less famous heroes. If we choose to accept our fate, we can be heroes in our world. The opportunity is out there and waiting for each of us to listen to the call for adventure.

At this point, you may wonder how far I am going with this and what time of night it was when I wrote it. I can assure you I don't mean mysticism, lightsabers, and magic. I am talking about the people in your company and *you* stretching beyond your current level of growth and achievement and facing the dragons that have held you back. I am talking about the millions of people stuck in a rut at work and not serving you or themselves to their full ability.

Real-World Dragons

Our dragons come in different sizes and natures, depending on the person. For example, some people are terrified of speaking up in a team meeting. Yet when they stay silent, we lose their potentially brilliant ideas. Some people are afraid of getting involved in a project because they will have to face new technology and they don't want to look stupid. Again, with their silence, we lose their contributions. Some leaders have dragons that manifest as fear to open themselves to the feedback they so desperately need to advance their careers and their leadership.

Each of the people above is facing a dragon, and each of these people can choose to be a hero when the call to adventure begins ringing in their ears. They can make themselves heroes, and we can help them.

Helping humans be heroes is more than an alliteration; it is a magic potion, secret weapon, red pill, and generous and noble way to help you and your team achieve amazing things at work.

One way to do this is through the successful application of technology paired with uniquely human skills. We can help humans be heroes through the successful use of Noble Automation, so let's explore how.

From Campbell's hero's journey, we can see the outline of successful patterns, both mythical and real. Every situation and character is different, but the pattern remains. We can help others to begin their journey and help our companies to thrive at the same time.

The Hero's Journey In Noble Automation

Phase One: The Separation

The first phase is helping your team, colleagues, or subordinates recognize that the current way the business functions may be uninspiring. You won't have trouble finding people who are not engaged. Remember, the truly engaged population is between 15 and 36 percent. Think about all that potential.

This is where Harry Potter sees that he can get out from under Dursley's stairs. It is where Luke sees he can leave the planet Tatooine. More importantly, this is where your employees see that they can leave the portion of their work that is frustrating, dull, error-prone, and discouraging and do the kind of work that fulfills them.

As a leader, you can help your team see that part of the way they are working is not the best use of their time, the path to their fulfillment, and certainly not heroic.

One way to do this is to show them samples of various tools to improve their lives. You probably don't want to sound anything like: "Look at the crappy way you work; it could be so much better." Though some do try this approach.

Once your team sees an inspired future, you can introduce them to a real-world Obi-wan Kenobi or Dumbledore, who can give them a clearer vision of the future and their capabilities. You are the guide here, the mentor, the wise sense of reason and hope. Remember Obi-wan Kenobi is not a threat to Luke in *Star Wars*, nor is Dumbledore to Harry Potter, nor Morpheus to Neo in *The Matrix*. They all genuinely want to see the protagonists succeed.

Phase Two: The Initiation

Phase two in the hero's journey requires trials and struggles. These are quickly found in tasking people to solve a difficult problem using tools they only barely understand. You can assure them that they learn the tools when the time comes, but like Socrates, you may want to lead them there with questions rather than answers.

Do you think your team does better with autonomy and the ability to solve their problems? Fortunately, since you likely don't yet know the best Intelligent Automation answer, trying to offer one will likely waste your time and demotivate your team. But if you give them the magic wand or the lightsaber (Intelligent Automation knowledge) and allow them to find the solutions, you may both be satisfied.

"I can't teach anybody anything. I can only make them think."
Socrates

Deep in the second phase, the hero struggles against adversity. Well-meaning helpers tend to arrive to bridge the gap, scale the wall, open the box, or in business get around the corporate bureaucracy that prevents much change. In the myths we all know, helpers tend to be specialists who provide what the hero needs to get out of their predicament.

In your company, these helpers may be technology experts or visits from people in other companies who have tackled similar problems. You can arrange for access to these people and make sure that they can help your team when they need it.

Facing The Dragon

No hero's journey is worthwhile until the protagonist faces their dragon. In Noble Automation, facing that dragon gets the project done by overcoming fear, resistance, and time. You can help by setting tough but achievable timelines and committing to compelling team rewards for meeting them. Inspiration comes from challenge. To be effective motivators, the schedule and rewards should be clear.

Phase Three: The Return

In the hero's journey, the return marks when the hero returns to his/her previous home as a changed person, perhaps with a physical prize like the sorcerer's stone from *Harry Potter*, or the one ring from *The Hobbit*. More often, in myth and reality, the hero returns with a transcendent experience that benefits the greater group. He/she slayed an internal dragon and gained knowledge that can't be taken away. Promotion? Bonus? Praise?

Now your team has arrived at the transformed future. They have solved a big problem by overcoming schedules, limitations, and deadlines; learned new technologies; and navigated company politics. They have faced dragons. They have also created something new and better that they fully support. In Noble Automation, this is likely the point where your project team has implemented something transformational and been recognized for it, and the celebration is over.

Now is when you support them with a communications team and plan worthy of their accomplishment. You can provide them the corporate bullhorn to explain to others what they have done, and *you* can be there to cheer them on when they are carried through the town square on the shoulders of the villagers. Think what can happen if each of the villagers not only cheers the team's success but longs for their own.

Phase Four: Reflection And Waiting For The Next Call To Adventure

After the project is complete, it is natural for the team members to settle into the new reality. For some team members, that will be just fine. After months of hard work and slaying dragons, they will need a break—a break you should give them.

For others, they will find the new norm no longer challenging, and they will seek a greater role and the next challenge. Could you help them find that role within your company or beyond?

Still, for others, the new world is alien, and they simply can't fit in. These people will need your HR team's help to find a new role via an empathic transition out of your company or department.

A common refrain from people who transition from companies is, "I should have left earlier." This comment is double-sided.

On one side, people who feel they should have left a particular company, job, or boss may have outgrown that position or reached a personality or style impasse that cannot be overcome. This person should have moved on.

On the other side are people who could have remained stimulated and eager to continue the journey in their company or role. Too often, they did not hear Campbell's phone ringing or receive the call to adventure, and perhaps their boss did not help them hear it either.

Beyond the human cost of this missed opportunity is the huge cost to the business. Hiring people is expensive and training them even more so. If an ounce of prevention is worth a pound of cure, then maybe we can all save a great deal of money by investing more early in helping the people on our teams be heroes in our business or beyond.

Everyone Can Be A Hero But Maybe Not In Your Company

For your company and some specific individuals to both succeed, you must part ways. Though this happens for different reasons, it is always challenging and sometimes painful. In the case of Noble Automation, the reasons someone may not fit in your future organization may be like the grocer mentioned before. He refused to keep his skills current until the world had passed him by.

In other cases, you may simply find that you no longer need as many people, or the people you need are different from those you have. This is where recognizing the nobility of work and the nobility of people is most important.

"Your toughest job is not hiring people but firing them. Even when in almost all cases they are miserable and they know it isn't working out, you still have to look them in the eye and tell them."
Brian Duperreault, Chairman, AIG[56]

"The day I don't lose sleep over layoffs is the day I step down."
CHRO, global toy company

Beyond making the final personnel decisions is the process, which in some cases is more important than the decision itself.

"How you do this, matters and it matters a lot.
These good, well-meaning people will be ambassadors
for your company when they leave and go into your community."
Roger Krone, CEO, Leidos[57]

Movies can be such a rich source of inspiration, and on this point, there is a scene from a 2009 George Clooney film, *Up in the Air*, that nails it.

Clooney plays a consultant who travels the world helping companies lay off people. There is an internal struggle between his colleague, a young consultant who thinks this can be done on the phone or video, and Clooney, the old-timer who knows the value of personal interaction.

The point comes to a head when Clooney and his young peer are laying off a twenty-five-year veteran. The clumsy young consultant incites rage from the employee about to lose his job: "Now what am I supposed to do to feed my family?"

Clooney, knowing the decision is final with no future role for the company veteran, reaches deeply into the man's background. Clooney notes that the man, while in college, had volunteered to work at a fine French restaurant rather than take a paid internship.

Clooney asks: "How much did they have to pay you here to give up your dream of being a chef?"

The tension disappears, and Clooney helps the man see his future, a delayed call to adventure waiting for him to answer.

I see Clooney's action as helping someone hear the phone and recognize the voice on the other side as a call to adventure. Each person must answer the phone themselves. You, the leader, can help them get there faster. You can help humans be heroes.

From each of the sixteen senior executives interviewed for this book came similar lessons, some painfully learned, on how to handle the departure of valuable people who no longer have a place in your company.

Best Practices For Helping People Be Heroes Outside Your Company

Treat People Like Human Beings
Give them the situation and the facts. Be direct and do not waffle on with extraneous words or facts. Remember, they are adults and want to be treated that way.

Seek First To Understand Them And Their Lives
Find out what is happening with that person holistically before you deliver the bad news. What is going on in their life? Listen.

Avoid The Empathy Trap
Recognizing what is happening in their lives or why they don't have the skills they need or what pressures they are under is essential to help you deliver the news. You still must deliver the news. "It's not personal; it's business."

Deliver The News At The Right Time, Place, And Circumstance
Every message has a better time to be delivered and a place to deliver it. Hint: just because you are ready to give the news doesn't mean they are ready to receive it.

Be Prompt
Whenever possible, deliver the news as soon as it is definite. Delaying the inevitable is bad for everyone, and word gets out. Cardboard boxes in the halls on Friday are poor form.

Treat Everyone With Respect
While everyone deserves human respect, you are doing this for two reasons: first, to treat the person well, and second, because your company and you will be judged in how you do this. Remember Roger Krone's words above.

Open Your Wallet
This is not a time to be cheap. Open your wallet and help the person and the situation move toward a better future.

The Golden Rule
Treat them like you would want to be treated.

Summary: Noble Automation Now Method Step Five

- Joseph Campbell was a leading global authority on mythology.

- He realized that intrinsic to our favorite myths and stories is the truth that each of our lives can be heroic or dreary.

- Most lives are dreary, partly due to the individual and partly due to the circumstances.

- Leaders have an opportunity with Noble Automation to succeed in their roles and help people feel like heroes in the process.

- To help someone be a hero means to help them stretch to be more of who they can be.

- Helping others in this way promotes great performance and loyalty to the leader and the cause.

- Leaders can help people be heroes in the company or to find their path outside the company.

Step Six: Operating Model Built For Purpose

The sixth step of the Noble Automation Now Method is to build your new automation implementation in a way that serves all your goals. This is often called an operating model. Like a great house, a Noble Automation implementation is something to be lived in, but at work.

To help crystalize this point, consider the colonial-style house, as common on the US East Coast as the traditional company organizational structure and change approach are in business. The colonial-style home goes back as far as the colonists arriving in North America in the 1600s. The command and control, top-down way of implementing change goes back at least to the Roman legions. There are parallels worth exploring.

The variations on the colonial-style home are all similar and easily recognizable. Most came from Europe. While outwardly attractive and originally functional, they were designed for a now antiquated lifestyle.

A typical colonial-style house is divided into many small rooms with a central or front hallway. Each room had its purpose, including the formal dining room, living room, family room, and kitchen on the ground floor and all bedrooms on the second floor. All of this may have made perfect sense in 1600, but in the twenty-first century, the design is fraught with inconveniences, wasted space, and awkward movements. Yet, the design prevails.

A typical command and control hierarchical and functional organization goes back to the early days of the military. Analogously, the typical change approach in companies depends on a formal structure, driven from the top down, and handed out to functional leaders and teams to implement.

Project team members are often chosen by who will cause the least disruption when taken from their work and not necessarily because they are the best resource for the project goal.

Frequently, in the early stage of the project, the team realizes that the problem they are trying to solve crosses functional lines, but the organization's leaders are vertically aligned. The challenges soon begin.

The modern American family doesn't live in the colonial house as it was designed. Similarly, innovative companies do not stay locked into formal hierarchical structures with rigid, clear, functional lines.

In the colonial house, most formal dining rooms and formal living rooms go empty much of the year. Yet, families feel obliged to protect the purpose of these rooms. They decorate them for the holidays and clean them. This effectively takes valuable space away from the way the family lives. So why do these homes continue to be built?

Similar questions can be asked about projects and change in organizations:
- Why do we tell the team what to do before we know what can be done?
- Why do we assemble the teams more functionally rather than horizontally to reflect the process being changed?
- Why do we choose people who may or may not have compatible work styles?
- Why do we insist that their solution fit into an existing organizational structure that may already be part of the problem?

The Most Obvious Question
Why do we ask teams to come up with a solution
that will result in one or more of them being let go?

These questions suggest there are better answers.

One memorable project included fixing a process that required several senior executive signatures on the critical path. These signatures had to be handwritten versus DocuSign or some other electronic tool we would use today.

Analysis of process delays pointed to signatures as a problem and delay. The elephant in the room was that the signatures required someone to walk to, you guessed it, the corner offices on several floors. Did the executives sit in these offices for a good business reason (like proximity to their teams)? No. They had corner offices because they were status symbols in this and many other companies.

If getting work done fast and using resources effectively is most important, decisions like corner office allocation would not get priority. With electronic signatures, this specific point is moot, but there are many more to consider when empowering our teams to change the world with Noble Automation.

Returning to home architecture, what perpetuates inefficient home styles? The answer is often momentum, risk aversion, and laziness. Many people simply don't think through how they will live and want to live before buying a house. In fact, most people buy houses based on street address, square footage, and of course, the kitchen. Often, only after they move in do they realize the inefficiencies of the typical colonial home. Years of expensive remodeling may follow.

American homebuilders didn't miss this outdated home design. From the 1950s, some builders began to make open-plan homes that had few walls separating the various rooms. These new designs effectively went from homes divided into small boxes to completely open homes. Innovation became a trend and people bought them. However, like a mad pendulum swinging from left to right, the new open plan had other extreme issues.

The analogy to this in a changing environment is when business leaders adopt some new fad or methodology without doing the deep dive to see if it will work in their company. Here are a few: quality circles, Six Sigma, open offices, delayering, management by objective, just-in-time inventory, 360 feedback (rarely stays private). Any one of these can be made to work and work well if the proper thought and planning are applied to implementing them. The chances only improve if consideration is given to the way the business works. This is not common enough.

The problem is that fully open-plan houses had too few walls or clear separation. This meant a loss of privacy and echoes from the free flow of sound. The builders had flip-flopped from tradition to fad. Neither solution recognized nor harmonized with the way people wanted to live. Frank Lloyd Wright was one man who understood this dilemma for buildings.

We earlier discussed how Wright set out to create and lead a school of architecture, not create different buildings lacking any consistent philosophy. A complete manifestation of Wright's leadership and principles was created in 1936 when the architect was sixty-five years old.

Perhaps you have visited Frank Lloyd Wright's masterpiece home Fallingwater in Bear Run, Pennsylvania. The 1936 home has been named the single most important architectural building in America by the American Institute of Architects.[58] Volumes have been written about this home, but the point here is that it was built with a vision and a plan, specifically for a particular family and their friends to enjoy the way they lived. Wright followed the robust principles he had created years before.

"I never design a building before I've seen the site and met the people who will be using it."
Frank Lloyd Wright[59]

Figure 7 Fallingwater Photo Christopher Little, Courtesy Western Pennsylvania Conservancy

The above quote is as simple as it is powerful. Beyond genius, what made Wright so special was his attention to aligning the building, purpose, environment, and owner. What made him so different was that he refused to build what others had built for no better reason than "that's the way it has always been built." The result of Wright's commitment to what he called organic architecture was buildings that were designed to do what they were meant to do and fit their environment. This is the inspiration for us with Noble Automation.

In Wright homes, this meant bypassing the bygone era of Victorian or colonial lifestyles with their servants and formality. Instead, he designed buildings that almost magically combined purpose, owner, and nature.

Noble Automation is a big opportunity to build a function or entire business that people want to work in like people wanted to live in Wright's Fallingwater. In this scenario, business leaders will apply the technology to solving business problems to maximize value to the customer and contributions from the employees, with the outcome being a robust and competitive business.

The rest of this step will discuss how you can be more like Frank Lloyd Wright and less like the local colonial-style tract homebuilder who keeps installing bathtubs too big to fill and rooms seldom used.

Building Lessons From The Noble Automation Front

Any big challenge can be divided into manageable pieces. This is how we humans do and build such wonderful and varied things. The questions for division are who, what, when, where, why, and how.

Why	For what compelling reasons are you doing this? What is the whole story, the one your team will figure out if you don't tell them and wonder why you didn't say it to begin with?
What	On what do you intend to focus Intelligent Automation? Are there boundaries? Any sacred cows (don't touch) parts of the business? What is already going on that may be connected?
Where	What parts of the business will be involved—specific countries, offices, functions, processes, products, or services? Work to be done virtually or face to face? A blend? Travel?
When	When do you want results, and why then?
Who	Who do you want involved in applying Intelligent Automation? Who will lead it? Who will approve it? Who will be on the team? Who will benefit from it? Who will determine success or failure?
How	What methodology are you following? Will you engage outside help? What technology are you willing to consider? How much are you willing to spend for what return?

Answering the above questions upfront is your metaphorical visit to the Fallingwater building site pre-construction. You, like Frank Lloyd Wright, won't know everything, but you will have a much better plan and a chance of succeeding.

Some Lessons From Automation

As young men or women, we bristled when our parents told us what to do. Mom or Dad would say: "I want you to make your own mistakes, just better mistakes than mine." On behalf of the contributors to this book, we would all like our teams to make their own decisions and mistakes, only not the same ones we made.

Let's Start With *Why* You Are Doing This

As Simon Sinek, author of *Start with Why*, says "why" is the most important question for success, motivation, employee engagement, and much more.[60] Perhaps asking: "What would motivate all the people who need to be involved in this to want to give it their all?"

To make sure our "why" is comprehensive, a framework called MECE (Mutually Exclusive Collectively Exhaustive) can help. MECE helps make sure we have covered all our bases. For "why" to be MECE, it should include good reasons to do this for all our stakeholders, written once, with nothing left out.

Good Practice: Communicate With A Clear Why

Leaders who communicate a clear vision that aligns with the organization's overall goals will avoid demoralizing internal conflict somewhere down the line.

MECE version:
- What is in it for the individual, otherwise known as WIFM, or what's in it for me?
- What is in it for the community or company?
- What is in it for the customer?
- What is the reason to do this and not something else or nothing at all?

Bad Practice: Make Poorly Informed Assumptions.

When the "why" is vague, our team likely won't give us the benefit of the doubt; rather, many will suspect our motives. We can't hide by being vague. We may think we are getting away with it, but we are guaranteeing less than 100 percent support.

What Should Your Focus Be?

Answering the what question means we have some idea where the opportunity lies in our company. We can get there knowing that a certain part of the company is fraught with manual tasks and generally inefficient. We may also not know where to start, which suggests some time spent on what technology exists to help. We may need to first engage the team to find the best "what" to choose. Our choice may depend on technology. Step 2 of this book is a good start to understand the technology.

Answering the what question also becomes political and psychological. Here are a few helpful questions:

- What parts of the business are most likely to adopt change?
- What parts are least likely to adopt change?
- What leaders are our change stars and who are our problems?
- What areas have the most cost?
- What areas, if improved, will give us the most competitive advantage?

Good Practice: Be Specific On The What

Clarify what we are trying to achieve as specifically as possible. This will be general, but with regular updates, should become clear and include the various parts of the company affected and not affected.

Bad Practice: Be Vague And Hope They Figure It Out

Letting the team navigate the politics of the business without our clear guidance or agreement as to what is in bounds and out of bounds is risky. Ignoring the team as they flip and flop around the business, being pushed by the soft or hard Machiavellian forces and power grabs in most organizations, is toxic. This is how Adolf Hitler managed Germany, and we know how that worked out.[61]

Where Will The Project Be Located?

Depending on the company's size, this can be an important or trivial point. In the earlier example of project disaster, the decision to do automation was made in one local European country, but the people directly impacted worked in other countries with different cultures and incentives. Reminder: it was an abject failure.

Good Practice: Be Specific And Involve The Right Locations

The people who will be involved need to be involved as early as possible, and this will likely have a big impact on help or resistance. We have all heard, "We are from headquarters, and we are here to help." We need to look carefully at the incentives of the people involved. More on that in the who section.

Bad Practice: Be Vague And Drop The Team Into Every Fire

Teams need focus, and they need boundaries, or success is elusive and resistance everywhere. Hoping the team will "sort it out" brings on that sick feeling at 3 a.m. when we know we didn't get involved enough or support the team with clarity. Sending people to the wrong countries or divisions can be a disaster.

When Will The Project Start And What Are The Milestones?

This is the easiest question once we know what you are trying to do and the scope of the project.

Good Practice: Start With A Target Date And Then Flex Once The Details Are Known

Beginning the project should align with the most significant goals of the company. Specifically, setting a scope for the first wave of improvements that will align with the way the company calendar works helps use the momentum of the natural organizational rhythm to support the project.

Starting with a high-level stretch target and a general goal is acceptable if the details come later. When the team comes back with an acceptable scope, we can align it to the company calendar (bonus time, fiscal year, vacation period), then we can set a firm target and stretch date. Hitting the target is good, but achieving the stretch goal is worthy of high praise and reward.

Bad Practice: Be Rigid As Steel Or Jiggly As Jell-O

Being too rigid from the first day is a recipe for failure. It assumes we know what we are trying to achieve before having enough information to set a realistic date. The concepts of target and stretch target will serve us better.

Who Will Be Involved?

The who question comes after why, what, where, and when for a good reason. Putting the right team together and assigning them the project we have outlined above is the most important decision we can make. This is likely no surprise to anyone reading this, but it still doesn't get the attention it deserves. Analogously, eating less and exercising more is the formula for weight loss, yet people ignore these points and seek silver bullets anyway. However, if succeeding with this project is essential, then team selection is critical.

Good Practice: Put The Right People In Charge And On The Team

If we put the people in charge who have a clear incentive to make sure this project succeeds and a healthy personal upside and unattractive downside, our chances improve. People perform at their best when the risk and reward are in balance.

The same can be said about incentives and the team, but individual skills should be the first consideration. Specifically, teams are not just several people who get thrown into a room and told they are a team. Good teams are people who have been selected for a balance of skills and personalities. This is where diversity moves from an abstract concept to a concrete reality. We need people who think differently and are compatible with the other team members.

There are several personality indicator tools with pros and cons to each. Myers Briggs Type indicator is a standard, and so are the Belbin team roles. Having your team complete the Gallup Strengths Finder is also helpful. A more obscure yet powerful tool relates to the various ways we humans innovate. The test is called a Kirton Adaption-Innovation Inventory. The outcome is to help teammates see how each other innovates.

Beyond personality types and innovation approaches are the obvious triumvirate required in any successful team member:

- First: they understand the businesses.
- Second: they can think in processes.
- Third: they get along with people.

Team members who are smart, ethical, and hard-working are the baseline.

Bad Practice: Put Little Thought Into Who Is Named To The Team

Assigning people to the team who are available rather than the right people for the task can be a recipe for disaster.

Finally, Let's Talk About *How* It Will Be Done

This book is about Intelligent Automation, which includes exciting technology and buzzwords like artificial intelligence, so why is this last? Because technology is the least important element of successful Intelligent/Noble Automation.

Good Practice: Make Educating Your Team On Tools A Priority

Deciding what tools to use for the business opportunity chosen is an iterative process. To begin, we must know what various technologies *can* do, and then we need to figure out where the best opportunities exist. Think of this like going into a Home Depot or Williams Sonoma, as mentioned in Step Two.

If you are doing a big home improvement project and already know exactly what you want to build and what tools you need, you are an experienced Home Depot shopper. You came in educated. The same with Williams Sonoma, the cooking store. When you walk into Williams Sonoma, you are likely overwhelmed with the desire to make something wonderful in the kitchen with all these cooking tools, but you don't know what you can make. Maybe you are then motivated but ignorant.

Intelligent Automation is like both these scenarios. Specifically, when your team knows the art of the possible with tools like robotic process automation, natural language processing, and image recognition, the world of opportunity is vast. However, if they only know a tool or two, their options are limited.

A better approach is to educate the team on tool capability, including lots of real-world examples. Then they can give you a suggested plan. The tools choice may well change the project direction. The needs of the business may dictate the tools. This is iterative. Once you find out how to use a pasta machine, you are off to the races making misshapen but tasty ravioli.

Bad Practice: Fail To Know All Your Tool Options

In a personal mea culpa, I was once called to help a telecoms client in Sweden understand the world of Intelligent Automation. I was familiar with and convincing about a small range of automation tools. I convinced the client that a tool I knew could solve their problems. I managed to sell the client on my suggestion. Congratulations, right? Wrong.

Over the next few months, I learned of another tool that had existed before I sold the first project but I was ignorant of. It was the better tool. I did not serve the client or the project well. My failure was not intentional or negligent; I just didn't know. I made this mistake because I did not know a full range of the art possible at the time.

Bringing It All Together

The previous sections covered who, what, when, where, why, and how. In a natural progression, you and your team are ready to get moving forward, but what is the next step?

To bring all this together and help you succeed, the following model and framework will reduce your risk, increase your chances of success, and help you sleep better at night. This is the Noble Automation Operating Model Framework, and it is the model I use to help clients succeed with Noble Automation.

The method is modeled on the two strands of DNA. Just as with DNA, if we break the strands apart, the DNA will fail to replicate, and biological life or Intelligent Automation business success will stop.

Unlike DNA, the framework is not rigid in sequence. We can go back and revisit portions again and then move forward with a new plan. Like DNA, however, in every project we do, without completing an important portion of the framework we are likely to create a form of mutation. In biological life, a mutation can be good, bad, or neutral. However, with enough mutations, the reproduction of the desired organism (successful project) will stop.

In Noble Automation, a mutation or deviation from the framework is a risk of subsequent projects being weaker and therefore less successful. A major deviation from a sound methodology or a DNA strand should be done with caution. The integration of leadership and implementation below is sound, tested, and proven in real life. That said, you may have a methodology that works better for you and your team. If your existing methodology is wanting, perhaps what is below will help fill any gaps.

INTELLIGENT AUTOMATION AND THE HERO'S JOURNEY

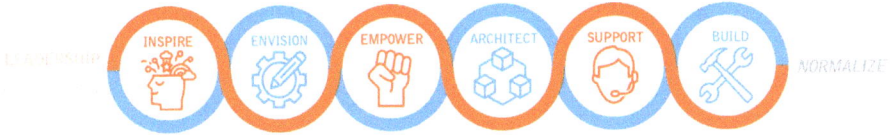

Inspire	Leaders must generate excitement and passion for the potential benefits of Noble Automation. This passion must address the hope and concerns of the business.
Envision	Noble Automation can mean many things to different people and companies. This phase is about shaping a business vision and potential use of technologies specific to your company, market, and team needs and capabilities.
Empower	Empowering the team with the knowledge of what they can do and what number of resources is the first part. Aligning their objectives, incentives, and careers is the second.
Architect	Like a building, your implementation of Noble Automation needs to have a plan that includes the plumbing (technology) and the floor layout (how it will be used daily). What, between a shack and Fallingwater, will you build?
Support	Properly empowered, educated, and rewarded, your team will create something of beauty if you support them through tangible demonstration of interest and barrier removal. This also includes rewards for success.
Build	Making the plan come to life requires building for purpose and keeping the team focused on business value. The first build will help show the way for the second, third, and fourth. The goal is a house of moveable bricks and not one of flammable straw.
Normalize	Change projects are often treated like vaccines. If a project of a particular type fails, then the naysayers will say, "We have tried that before." Normalizing means building a sense of inevitability for more projects; some will be big successes while all will be lessons.

The IES-EAB Methodology™ above is designed for the whole team and speaks to the various phases of work. The hero's journey is personal and will differ for each of the people on your team. You can imagine that treating everyone as if they are at the same point in their career or life would come across at the least as awkward and disingenuous at the worst.

Closer to ideal is to treat every person on the team as being on their own journey. It is how they feel, so why not speak directly to them?

Step 5 discussed the case for how we as leaders can help humans be heroes while implementing the tools and technologies of Intelligent Automation. As a reminder, the three phases of the hero's journey are separation, initiation, and return.

Below is where those phases apply in the team level practical business of accomplishing Noble Automation transformations.

INTELLIGENT AUTOMATION AND THE HERO'S JOURNEY

Summary: Noble Automation Now Method Step Six

- Implementing Noble Automation is like building a house: we can follow outdated design ideas because they are traditional or build something that will beautifully serve its occupants.

- Clarity around the who, what, when, where, how, and why will pay off massively going forward.

- Successful implementation means combining leadership and project implementation like the strands of DNA. The IES-EAB Methodology™ has worked before and should complement your existing best practices.

- Implementing technology can be dull; a project to help our teams live, work, and feel like heroes can be electrifying. Which would you rather be?

Step Seven: Aligned Incentives And Culture

*"Only through struggling, labor, and risk
are great accomplishments realized."*
Alexander the Great

Any reader of this book has likely survived a significant company change. Unless you've had the pleasure and pain of leading one of these transformations, you may have kept your head low and moved on with your job. Most major changes fail, but some defy the odds, are successful, and become a much better way to work and succeed. Why is that?

A quick trip through Amazon for change management books is overwhelming. Famous academics have built careers on change, yet the odds remain globally low. Another entire generic change management book is probably not the solution.

What follows is a mercifully short and focused summary of a successful change approach for Noble Automation. It combines the classic people, process, and technology elements with helping humans be heroes. The approach also highlights the specific challenges and opportunities of Noble Automation.

This **step** combines personal experience and executive interviews for a total of 450 years of corporate experience. Please take what you find valuable from both and combine it with what has worked for you.

The change you are going to make has three dimensions—people, process, and technology—listed in the order of complexity.

People: Your colleagues need to be motivated, informed, empowered, and secure that working on your vision is good for them. When the crucial initial project is complete, they need to believe that there is no way of going back—"the ships are burned."

Process: The business process changes from automation need to be clear and helpful for all those who use them. Once in place, the other processes in the company need to support the new way of working and encourage more advances in automation.

Technology: The new technology needs to be implemented, stable, and open to the necessary maintenance required. Paradoxically, the technology must also remain open to future changes.

To sustain the changes and hopefully accelerate with additional improvements, the groundwork must be laid well before the "go live" date.

If you remember back in Step Five, where we talked about the hero's journey and then linked it to the IEE-ASB Methodology, you can see change management's role.

The three hero's journey stages again are separation, initiation, and return. Using these same stages, you can successfully navigate the journey to Noble Automation.

The table below shows aligns the hero's journey and the two essential threads of Noble Automation success, specifically leadership and implementation.

The combination provides a useful, simple framework that is not overly academic.

Stages in the Change Journey		
Hero's Journey	Separation	Initiation	Return
Leadership	Inspire	Empower	Support
Implementation	Envision	Architect	Build

Leadership Change Imperatives

Inspire: To inspire means to "arouse by divine influence" in some dictionaries. While not divine, you are the leader or department manager of your team.

Your goal is to inspire your team to willingly "separate" from the past on a journey to the future. People want to be inspired, and they want to see their work matter at a higher level. Do you want to be inspired? Turn off the cynicism knob if you must, but isn't being inspired wonderful?

Critical ingredients include an inspiring, clear, and memorable vision; a team of engaged colleagues; and the personal security of knowing that this project will not derail their careers.

Empower: Empowerment is another way of saying you provide the team what they need to get the job done. That something includes the people, access, resources, authority, and hard-to-measure gravitas required to do something difficult and potentially disruptive. Far too many leaders think we have empowered the team but never validate that the team feels empowered. See Step 5.

Test: If you have not had someone from the team ask you for support somehow, there are only two options. Either you gave them everything they need, or they are hesitant to ask you. Asking how you can help is gold.

Support: People know when leadership support is pro forma or when the boss finds the work genuinely worthy of celebration. Showing up and saying some puffery never impressed me much; how about you?

When the boss takes time to talk about the project or initiative and then follows through with the kind of rewards (tangible and intangible) that make employees feel special, the team is moved. Money, in the form of a bonus or raise, is just icing on the cake.

The secondary value of sincere celebrations is the effect on observers. When others see the celebration and senior-level attention, they want to join the party and the next project.

Implementation Change Imperatives

Envision: When adopting new technologies like those in Intelligent Automation, it is easy for us to aim too small or narrow. Sometimes this overly conservative scope is caused by limited technology understanding, the "I only have a hammer" syndrome. Robotic process automation, for example, is powerful but more so when combined with other tools.

An overly limited scope chosen for automation can also reflect the team's limited understanding of how the larger business works. Automating one small area may have no significant impact, where automating a whole process flow could unleash big potential.

The envisioning process at its best includes a good, healthy dose of bold innovation powered by awareness of what is possible and built to complement what is currently done.

Here are three ways successful teams have created meaningful scope.

1. Assure the team knows how the chosen business area works and why.
2. Help them understand what pain/irritation/waste is felt by those in the business and especially the customers affected by it.
3. Broaden the team's understanding of what can be done and what has been done in other companies; let the team's genius be released on your business.

Note: *Genius* may sound like hyperbole, but you have likely experienced results of a highly effective and empowered team that reflected a kind of genius.

Architect: This is all about combining what the user wants with no limitations and what is possible. For example, what huge improvements could be achieved if traditional business/organizational boundaries evaporated?

Many inefficient or ineffective processes result from teams trying to make solutions fit a current organization or, more sadly, an office floor plan layout. (COVID may change this forever.) The teams often suggest what is required to survive in the current culture. Perhaps the more promising opportunity is to help them think boldly outside the current boundaries. We are on the right track when teams start with sentences with "What if...."

The value and risk of the craftsman: Transformation teams often have a technology craftsman of sorts who, for good reasons, joins the group. Craftsmen are handy people, but some tend to create from scratch rather than work with existing tools and resources. Another key element is to help them see how wonderful a good solution implemented can be versus a perfect solution left on the whiteboard.

We should keep an eye out for both the craftsman and the perfectionist.

Build: Success in the build phase sometimes rides on helping the technology team members not involved in the specific project feel comfortable with the new process and technology. Building their comfort lowers resistance caused by ignorance and fear of personal obsolescence. Most importantly, it increases buy-in for current and future projects.

Nobody wants to be known as the "expert of the old." An iconic example comes from Steve Jobs' tenure as Apple CEO. Jobs reportedly disparaged the programmers keeping the Apple II machines (the past) running as he worked to roll out the Macintosh (the future). Both were required to keep the company profitable, but Jobs was insensitive to the feelings of the old guard, and it cost the company in morale and energy.

Let's let Steve Jobs be a role model to us all in his best and worst traits. You need the whole team for the future, and the best way to keep the old guard motivated is to help them feel valued and part of the future.

Finally, build includes creating the new behaviors required to support ongoing automation adoption and success. These include communications, rewards, career paths, and organizational operations that will support the growing vision.

Change Lessons From The Intelligent Automation Front Lines

To avoid becoming a case study of failure, and rather, become a lesson in success, we can all learn from what has happened elsewhere. The examples below come from specific clients and projects suggested to me by the executives interviewed for this book, my consulting colleagues, and my experience over thirty years.

Before The Project

Develop a clear, complete, and compelling vision of what you want from implementing Noble Automation. Test how clear your vision is by filling in this sentence:

> "We at [your company] are moving forward with Noble Automation in [fill in business area] because we see the great potential to improve how we serve our customers and compete in the market.

> "We expect the benefits to include [your project specifics], which we will measure by improvements in [your metrics].

> "We know that adopting new technology like this can be disruptive and unsettling, so we are going to communicate openly and early as we understand what effect this will have on our business and colleagues.

> "While we cannot guarantee the future now, we can guarantee we will treat all our colleagues with respect and fairness, regardless of whether their jobs will change, remain the same, or be outside our company."

Test how well your message is received by asking your people to repeat it.

Alan Colberg, CEO of Assurant, a risk management products and services company with $10B+ revenue and $45B+ billion in assets, told me how important the vision is to have his 14,000 people rally around change. His vision for Assurant is four simple and powerful points:

Customer focus: Understand what the customer wants, needs, and would want if they knew they could have it.

Adaptation: Embrace, accept, and pursue change to serve the customer better. This naturally includes technology and helps the company move forward with automation and other plans.

Diversity of thought and inclusion: Alan emphasized that Assurant draw out the best of his teams to adapt and serve customers. The best way to do this is actively seek out diversity in both thinking and experience and include everyone in the process.

Long-term enterprise value: Alan's focus is beyond his tenure and that of his current employees. The vision is to build a company that will provide value to future customers, employees, and stakeholders.

With a vision like this integrated into every training course, incentive plan, and performance review, Alan is well-positioned to take advantage of all Intelligent Automation offers.

During The Project

An Intelligent Automation project will change the company—specifically, the way people work. Organizations, like people, resist change. Only with steady and unrelenting support will they succeed.

The naysayers in your organization are like water flowing with gravity. They will find any crack, gap, crevice, or opportunity to get through. For Noble Automation or any other significant change, these gaps manifest as statements made by leaders that waver from support. Rather than providing examples of these statements, the key is what the leader thinks. If the leader believes in the project, he or she won't find themselves "slipping up."

If you squeeze an orange, you will get orange juice. If you squeeze a leader who does not support a change, you will get half-hearted statements of support or outright dismissals of the initiative. To the naysayers and Machiavellians in the company, these are clear signs that this program is vulnerable, like a weak gazelle on the savanna is to the hungry lion.

Part of this support is establishing how Noble Automation will be carried on after implementation. This is your deployed vs. build operating model.

A recent thought piece from McKinsey and Company says full-scale and growing automation initiatives shape how businesses operate. They see operating models effectively evolving with automation as a core driver and not a peripheral activity.[62]

After The Project

The opportunity for failure is greatest when the project is starting and second greatest when it finishes. The naysayers, or simply the people who don't like the new change, will fight like hell to go back to the old ways. Because of this, leaders must continue to support the new approach with questions about progress, rewards for achieving goals, public signs of support, and a sense of the inevitability of the next related change.

This is where an ongoing operating model is so important. An operating model is a fancy way of saying how you are going to organize the business to answer four questions:

1. How will the newly completed automation be used and maintained?
2. How will the completed automation be updated to reflect new business needs?
3. How will new automation ideas be put forward, approved, and put into action?
4. Who will do what? Accountabilities, responsibilities, involvement.

Developing operating models is where strategy crosses the line to operations. This can be fraught with pain if people who see themselves only as strategists write operational approaches. Instead, when the project is complete, it is time for a smooth handoff to the operational team to refine the operating model and run the transformed business.

Of course, not every project will naturally rise in interest to the level of the CEO, but is that a mistake? While the CEO does not need to know every project in detail, the ROI (return on investment) of having the CEO aware enough of the projects to offer praise is one of the highest returns an executive can get. The effect of pizzas or sushi sent to a late-working team by the CEO can't accurately be measured.

In a personal example that changed my career forever, Jack Welch (GE's CEO) once stood with my project team and me for fifteen minutes, asking about what we had done. He was genuinely interested and asked good questions. Jack had many other priorities to spend his time on, but he chose to spend time with us. We would have crawled through broken glass for him. Such is the power of change management and leadership.

While much more can be done to assure successful change, the Pareto Principle applies. Specifically, you get 80 percent of the value from 20 percent of the steps. I'm suggesting the list above includes 20 percent of the actions that will give you 80 percent of the value.

Summary: Noble Automation Now Method Step Seven

- Organizations and individuals struggle with change. The people suggesting the change find it exciting, while those being asked to change find it threatening.

- A culture that supports change and recognizes that it is challenging is a great early step.

- Aligning the incentives for the individual and teams to support the desired change is a good idea and one often overlooked.

- Leaders can be helped by thinking of their actions to enable a hero's journey in their teams. Each phase benefits from specific actions and proven practices.

PART FOUR

Facing Your Dragon

"I've had a lot of worries in my life, most of which never happened."
Mark Twain[63]

The hero's journey is a common outline for great movies and books; Joseph Campbell asserted that beyond entertainment, the hero's journey is a metaphor for our lives. Further, since we all spend most of our waking time pursuing our vocation, many of our most exciting adventures will or could happen at work.

Noble Automation will, for many of us, be a great adventure if we choose to take it. There is the potential for great excitement, the possibility of business and personal success, and at the least, the need to grow and experience the future. All in all, this has the making of an exciting journey, perhaps you and your team's next adventure.

In analyzing the adventures you have already taken, you may discover what Campbell found. Specifically, while everyone gets the call for the hero's journey repeatedly in their lives, many of us refuse to answer the phone and act. Despite the inner voice telling us we want the adventure and need the adventure to be who we are capable of being, we hesitate.

The reasons we tell ourselves are as diverse as we are and often include:
"That is too hard."
"Nobody at my age does that."
"I have never seen someone like me do something like that."
"If I do that, I will fall off the promotion track."
"What would people I respect say if I tried that?"

There are many more reasons or excuses where these came from. However, digging behind these, we likely find fear the chief reason we hide from the call to adventure.

Drill sergeants often describe fear as false evidence appearing real. When evaluated in broad daylight, the facts and likely outcomes of accepting the next call to adventure suggest we exaggerate negative possibilities. Simultaneously, we minimize positive possibilities. This feels like a great avoidable tragedy of human nature.

In Campbell's research, the dragon is what we project outside ourselves as the biggest barrier to our success. The dragon in Western mythology is chosen because it is the biggest, "baddest," and scariest of all monsters; after all, what other than the biggest monster could prevent us from achieving our dreams?

The truth, however, is that the dragon most of us face is fear. We project outward the image of a bigger and "badder" monster than we feel capable of beating to give us an excuse not to act. What kind of fool messes with a fire-breathing dragon?

Archetypes

Archetypes are imperfect, but they help frame the discussion around common and familiar characteristics, roles, or issues the group faces.

When we realize the dragon is fear and that fear is holding us back, we can overcome it. We can answer the call to adventure; complete the three phases of the hero's journey; and bring to our tribe, team, or household the treasures of our newfound wealth or experience.

The specific implications of Noble Automation are different for everyone in every vocation and therefore beyond accurate generalization. However, some archetypes are useful.

For the implementation of Noble Automation, five archetypes are common:

- The CEO/COO
- The CIO/technology leader
- The HR or people leader
- The business (P&L) manager/leader
- The Noble Automation project leader
- The individual employee or team member

Each of these are important roles, and we, as individuals, face unique challenges.

The CEO/COO

The Call To Adventure

You have worked hard to get to this position. You have overcome many obstacles, including the market, the economy, competitors, and most importantly, yourself. Well done. Money, while important, is not your primary motivator. More likely, your mission is to make things better for your company, family, and community now and into the future. You want to leave a legacy.

Helpful Questions

Would leading your company again into something bold like Noble Automation help you achieve your big goals? Do you see the potential in a Noble Automation transformation as what your company needs?

Your Dragon

It is likely lonely at the top of your organization, as it seems to be for many top leaders. Every decision you make is scrutinized by your company, the markets, and your peers. To fail to act is fraught with risk, but so is acting recklessly.

Thought-Provoking Questions

Can you succeed with this new technology and find the next vein of success for your company, or will this derail your plans? What happens if you simply do something else? What if that fails?

The Treasure

If automation even approaches the current level of hype, it will change the game. Your employees will have an exciting and rewarding experience. Some will finally be able to invest their precious human skills into their careers and your company. Some will leave. Ultimately, if your company thrives, many boats will rise in the tide.

CIO / Technology Leader

As the executive responsible for your company's technology, you know it is your team that keeps the machine running. You also know that competition increasingly depends on your staying current with new capabilities. You must balance innovation and stability.

The Call To Adventure

This new technology and particularly the combination of multiple types of technology could represent a major advance for your company. You and your team could embrace and implement tools that leave your competition in the dust and help your company thrive. It could be exhilarating.

Helpful Questions

Where can you use these tools? How will they help your current plans? Which of these tools could best accelerate your goals? What do you need to know?

Your Dragon

What if all these shiny new technology balls are a passing fad or worse yet make your core systems and processes unstable? What if they fail? What if this is a huge waste of money?

Thought Provoking Questions

Do you feel the sense of inevitably of some or many of these technologies? How can this be a major step forward in how you serve the business and demonstrate your value at a whole new level? How exciting could this be? What if you do nothing?

The Treasure

The technology teams that embrace the right tools for their business have the potential to step far out in front of the competition. Technology leaders who show that they are open to innovation and change like this attract and retain top talent. Leaders like these grow personally and professionally.

The HR (People) Leader

The Call To Adventure

As the leader directly tasked with the most valuable assets of your company, you are on the lookout for every way to help your people succeed. Millennials are looking for meaning at work and are quick to run from mundane tasks and distant leaders. You are the CEO's business partner, and he/she relies on you to draw out the best of the business.

Helpful Questions

Does Noble Automation give you a chance to help the employees grow and become more of who they can be while the company succeeds? Does the challenge of helping the business adopt new skill sets, tools, and working styles excite you? Does the promise of more human work resonate with your goals and those of your company?

Your Dragon

This could all go wrong, and parts of this are outside your comfort zone and expertise. There is great personal and professional risk here. You are an HR leader, not a tech person. Do you understand this?

Thought-Provoking Questions

What will happen when automation becomes a bigger subject in your company? How will you balance the fear that many will feel with the promise of new, better, and faster? What if you fail to manage the change and end up losing key people? What happens if you don't act and the company suffers?

The Treasure

As an HR/people leader, you have a slightly maternal or paternal role. What do the people of your company want you to do? How can you deliver as a partner to the C-suite? If you add Noble Automation and keep your top talent, does this meet a top priority? This will certainly expand your skills and likely add to your legacy and satisfaction.

The Business Manager

The Call To Adventure
You are responsible for a portion of the business and the team that makes it work. You likely face an ongoing challenge to motivate your team while pushing them to ever-improving performance.

Helpful Questions
Do you have existing tools that will get you where you need to go, or do you need a breakthrough? Do Noble Automation and a team working to be their true selves excite you enough to act?

Your Dragon
Time is tight already, and maybe you don't have time for another initiative. Maybe you can make your numbers and retain your team without automation. What if this derails your fragile situation?

Thought-Provoking Questions
Do you have a better way to succeed and meet your numbers? How can you get up to speed and get ahead of this?

The Treasure
This could change the game in your department and result in your best people using their best human traits to do great work. You could save money, delight customers, and polish your accomplishments and skills at the same time. You will likely become more confident through your new skills, accomplishments, and financial success. What could be next in your career?

The Noble Automation Project Leader

The Call To Adventure
This could be that career-boosting project that makes you wake up early and go to sleep late. This could be a chance to lead a team through difficult work and produce results that mean something to your business. You are always looking to grow and doing so with cutting-edge technology could be exhilarating.

Helpful Questions
Is your job already rewarding and stimulating enough? Do you want something exciting to work on? Is Noble Automation a big thing or just another thing to you?

Your Dragon
Big projects are risky and will likely take you away from your routine and comfort zone. Maybe that's a good thing, but it is still risky. If you keep your head down, it won't get taken off. Then again, you won't see opportunities if you are staring at your shoelaces. If you fail, you may never get to lead anything else again.

Thought-Provoking Questions
What if this fails? What if this is some special project that derails your whole career in the company? What if leadership is not there to support you? What if you can't handle the work and the team won't follow you? Is there any more exciting work you would prefer to do?

The Treasure
This could be the project that takes your career forward as you have always wanted. Yes, it is a big responsibility and a calculated risk that only you can make. You could work with great people and together get better.

The Individual Employee/Team Member

The Call To Adventure
This could be that super exciting project that takes you away from your routine and gives you a chance to make the business better and to put actions to the thoughts you have had for a while. This could also be a chance to shine and show the company how much more you can offer, maybe even get a promotion? At the least, you will ride an exciting wave of change and technology. The worst thing that could happen is you take the new skills somewhere else. The best thing is you grow and succeed in a place with people you respect.

Helpful Questions
Have you been waiting for a change to do something new and exciting? Do you have a better opportunity to grow?

Your Dragon

This could go terribly wrong, and the team members may be blamed for a leadership misstep. You may not be able to learn what you need to know.

Thought-Provoking Questions

What if you can't understand this new technology? What if this is just some special project that derails your whole career in the company? What if the team leader is not there to support you? What is he/she takes all the credit, and you work for nothing?

The Treasure

This is how you can grow, succeed, and be happier at work and in life. You will be stretched and come out the other side as a more competent and confident person.

Summary: Facing Your Dragon

- Most people lead lives of quiet desperation, and your company is no different.
- Most people long for adventure and an interesting life.
- The primary barrier to growth and success is fear.
- Joseph Campbell tied the mythical dragons of literature to the inner fear of failure in humans.
- Every role in your company and every person in those roles has fears and dragons.
- You can help yourself, your peers, and your colleagues face their fears and overcome them with Noble Automation.

PART FIVE
Conclusion

If you have written a book, you may agree with Ernest Hemingway:

> "There is nothing to writing, all you have to do
> is sit down to a typewriter and bleed."
> **Ernest Hemingway**[64]

First, I am not Hemingway. Second, I used a computer. Nonetheless, the bleed part is metaphorically true. Aside from the effort it takes to write, ask yourself repeatedly why you are writing this book and why a busy leader would want to read it. Specifically, are you creating something of value to the world or trying to make yourself feel good? In all candor, it is both.

My first book, *Placing Stones: Doing and Having What Matters Most*, was about young professionals' intense struggle trying to balance life's priorities. The subject was deeply personal, and the process of writing it, specifically seeking others' input, profoundly helped me find my balance with work, family, fitness, and personal development.

This book serves a similar purpose and comes from a personal place. Work, in my view, is noble and working with other people, growing, overcoming limitations, struggling, and finding success, big or small, is one of life's great rewards. This reward is often fleeting and absent due to leadership failings we can change, specifically those addressed in this book.

Intelligent Automation elevated to Noble Automation is an incredible opportunity to make work more rewarding. Intelligent Automation is a series of waves with energy built up from far away and waiting for us to have the courage to swim out, stand up, and enjoy the ride.

As our careers unfold and the years pass, we realize we have a limited number of waves to ride before our professional journeys end. You've likely had incredible rides and maybe some spectacular crashes. I've had both. While important to reflect on, there is no time to look back because the next set is here.

So, with the sun shining, the water warm, the waves arriving, you and I have everything we need for a magnificent ride—a hero's journey toward becoming more of our noble selves.

See you out there!

Chris

Christopher Hodges

APPENDIX A

Deep Dive: Leadership for Noble Automation

Step 1 provided a brief overview of the Baldrige Award criteria for great businesses. This section goes deeper for leaders looking to refresh or enhance their approach to building a great company and team.

Intertwined in the examples below is the most important success factor of leaders. It is that *je ne sais quoi* or difficult to describe combination of qualities that make people want to follow you and me. Truly great leaders have a focus on both these general criteria and their personal *je ne sais quoi*.

Baldrige Criteria: Systems Perspective

A systems perspective means managing all the parts of your organization as a unified whole to achieve your mission and strive toward your vision.

Leadership Example

Laurent Freixe is executive vice president and CEO of the Americas for Nestlé, leading the largest region of the world's number one food and beverage company. With a team of 70,000 associates, he leads a business accounting for more than 2,500 brands, ranging from global icons to local favorites, present across Canada to Chile.

In his extended leadership team, he collaborates with over fifteen nationalities, bringing a wealth of diverse experiences, cultures, and skills, working together to win in the marketplace and to create shared value for Nestlé's stakeholders. Freixe recognizes the importance of a strong team, paired with powerful strategies and resources to invest, to succeed in today's marketplace. He further acknowledges that his constituents include his employees, his customers, and the communities they operate in and serve.

Figure 8 Nestlé Strategic Virtuous Circle Award - Artist Glenda Léon, La Habana and Madrid. Courtesy Nestlé

To crystalize the importance of this symbiotic relationship, Freixe developed the Strategic Virtuous Circle, Nestlé's management model, to ensure sustainable and profitable growth while creating value. It is built in four phases, governed by a core of sustainability and people necessary for the model to last.

Freixe recognizes that every year is different, and he wants to encourage his team to strive toward success, accelerate growth, and sustainably win in the marketplace. For this reason, he has created the Strategic Virtuous Circle trophy to be awarded annually to those markets with the strongest contribution.

To keep the award fresh and desirable, he commissions an artist to design a different sculpture every year, always maintaining the shape of a virtuous circle to reflect the values he knows to make the company successful. See Figure 8[65].

Freixe has allowed me to share his management model of performance with you. Here is how he describes the importance of the circular shape and performance dimensions.

"Our business must focus first on efficiency and productivity including Lean and Process Improvement. The savings are then used to invest in growth and innovation. Profitable growth enables us to support our people and protect the environment more fully. The people are again in the center and the wheel turns again. It is truly a virtuous circle."

Laurent Freixe, Nestlé CEO, Americas

Laurent Freixe, Nestlé[66]

Implications For Intelligent Automation:

- Is the capacity of your various teams balanced so that work is not stuck in bottlenecks?
- Are the incentives for the various parts of your company contradictory and effectively driving unnecessary conflict, or are they aligned end to end?
- Do your various units work together toward a common goal or fight internally for recognition?
- Is your team rewarded for your version of a virtuous circle?

Baldrige Criteria: Visionary Leadership

Your organization's senior leaders should state a vision, create a customer focus, demonstrate clear and visible organizational values and ethics, and set high expectations for the workforce.

Leader Making This Real Today

Roger Krone, CEO of Leidos, is a forty-year veteran of corporate America. He has worked in some of America's biggest and most successful companies, including Boeing, McDonald Douglas, and General Dynamics. Taking on his current role in 2014 as CEO of Leidos (43,000 employees), Krone entered a new phase of his career.

Specifically, Leidos has a long and successful history as an employee-owned company. Krone recognized that when Leidos changed structures and became a publicly listed company, there was a risk that the employee ownership mindset would dissipate. He and his leadership team knew that the business required visionary leadership and values that were respected in the past to drive the future.

To avoid losing the magic of Leidos, he and his team worked hard and long to produce the vision, purpose, and values that would inspire the business going forward. The result is a four-part, short, and focused statement of what and who Leidos is.

When I pressed Krone on how he makes sure this is imbued into the daily work, he gave me several examples. Starting early, Krone meets face-to-face or virtually every Monday with the company's new employees. In these sessions, he walks through the Leidos values below and provides real work-related examples of what they look like in action.

I asked him how he would handle his words being ignored and people not following the company values even when given by the CEO. He confirmed that while the process is rare, Leidos separates people who do not follow the mission, vision, and values, sending an important signal about what matters. This double-sided commitment at Leidos is as powerful as it is rare, except, of course, in the world's great companies.

Mission, Vision, And Values Of Leidos

Everything we do is built on a commitment to do the right thing for our customers, our people, and our community. Our mission, vision, and values guide the way we do business.

Mission
- Leidos makes the world safer, healthier, and more efficient through technology, engineering, and science.
- Become the global leader in the development and application of technology to solve our customers' most demanding challenges.

Vision
- Engage, develop, and empower our diverse and valued people to foster a culture of creativity and growth.
- Strengthen our communities through volunteerism, sustainable operations, and the advancement of diversity and inclusion.

Values

Integrity	• Is having the courage to make tough ethical decisions, taking pride in our work, being transparent with our team, and being respectful of everyone.
Inclusion	• Is fostering a sense of belonging, welcoming all perspectives and contributions, and providing equal access to opportunities and resources for everyone.
Innovation	• Is not limited to our engineers and scientists. It is acting as a catalyst. Being tenacious and curious to help us excel and be a part of a learning organization.
Agility	• Is being flexible, creative, and resilient. It is our ability to think and act small while using the size and strength of our balance sheet to our advantage.
Collaboration	• Is being team-oriented and proactively engaging to meet shared objectives. It is about building relationships and staying connected with each other.
Commitment	• Is being accountable, taking ownership, modeling servant leadership, and operating with a sense of urgency to our customers and teams.

Implications For Intelligent Automation:

- Do your employees know what your mission and vision are? Could they describe them?
- Is the vision inspirational? How do you know?
- How do you handle those who do not support your vision, ethics, or expectations?

Baldrige Criteria: Customer-Focused Excellence

Your customers are the ultimate judges of your performance and product and service quality. Thus, your organization must consider all product and service characteristics and modes of customer access and support that contribute to customer satisfaction, loyalty, positive referrals, and ultimately, your organization's ongoing success.

Leader Making This Real Today

Raina Moskowitz is the chief operations, strategy and people officer for Etsy, the online marketplace for more than four million independent sellers of handmade and vintage items. In this role, she has the unique challenge of keeping three essential customer constituencies happy to drive business excellence.

Her job is to focus on her customers (millions) and her seller community (four million) and find ways to help them thrive together. The third side of her triangle of opportunity is to motivate her internal team to stay energized and focused while growing rapidly.

What I found both unique and inspiring from speaking with Moskowitz was how she had established communication channels, seller outreach, and support mechanisms for all three groups. She intrinsically recognizes "they are all in this together," specifically Etsy's vision to "make commerce human."

Three standout points show Etsy's customer-focused excellence:

First is their comprehensive feedback solicitation and follow-up for end-use customers. This is particularly important given that many of Etsy's sellers are "mom and pop" sized businesses without extensive operations infrastructure. Etsy needs to know how its buyers are served.

Second is Etsy's commitment to seller success, including outreach and support to sellers struggling to succeed and maintain Etsy's high standards. Moskowitz's team has a multi-pronged approach to support these struggling stores and make them successful.

Third, Moskowitz provides her internal team the support they need to keep the sellers successful. She describes this as building resilience and focusing on "the good of the commons." In practice, to create a vibrant marketplace, the Etsy team occasionally needs to part ways with a seller who simply can't serve the clients to Etsy standards.

The success of Etsy, its sellers, and its employees depends on good experiences with the buyers. Without internal processes and a supportive leadership team, Etsy employees would be torn from two sides and unlikely to succeed.

Implications For Intelligent Automation:

- How do your customers view your company?
- How will you ensure they are not negatively impacted by your adoption of Noble Automation (think endless phone trees with no humans)?
- Do you focus on all your customer groups to achieve business excellence?

Baldrige Criteria: Valuing People

A successful organization values its workforce members and the other stakeholders, including customers, community members, suppliers, partners, and other people affected by your actions.

Leader Making This Real Today

Kimo Kippen, former VP of global work initiatives at Hilton and leadership learning officer at Marriott, has spent his career focused on the value of people. He shared with me what he believed was the most powerful people-valuing culture he has experienced was Marriott. Kippen cited several examples of how the company was infused with the people-first value from training to promotion and departure. I am a Platinum Elite traveler with Marriott (away from home too much) just for this reason.

The hotel chain is legendary for its founders and the chain of family members who have led and owned the company. Marriott is driven by the philosophy of its founder, J. Willard Marriott, and his son Bill, and it percolates throughout the more than 120,000 employees. The ethos served the company well during the decades of growth, and it served them well during the downturn of COVID, though the pain in hospitality has been extreme.

At the core of the organization's success is a three-step virtuous cycle (sounding familiar?), which begins with the associates.

Marriott Founder's Philosophy
- Take care of the associates and they will take care of the customers.
- Happy customers lead to more happy customers.
- Market share follows and so does profitability.

Again, it would be easy to say that these are only words, but after eighty-five years in business and a long list of awards and recognition for being a great workplace, Marriott deserves the credit for being a company that truly values people.

Implications For Intelligent Automation:
- How valued do your people feel? How do you measure that, and what do you do to improve it?
- How will you handle reductions in people from Intelligent Automation?

Baldrige Criteria: Organizational Learning And Agility
Organizational learning includes continuous improvement of existing approaches and significant change or innovation, leading to new goals, approaches, products, and markets. Organizational learning must allow for agility, a capacity for rapid change, and flexibility in operations.

Leader Making This Real Today

"Organizations that embrace a culture of learning create an environment that encourages curiosity and knowledge sharing, which in turn leads to better business outcomes."
Google[67]

Google is legendary for the time and effort they put into learning and agility. The phrase "Learning is a right at Google" comes to mind. Google has also been on the best one hundred companies to work for list eight out of eleven years.

Google makes learning a core part of employment. They do this through lectures from the leading minds in the world. They focus on the impact and effectiveness of the training and lectures by rating the sessions and culling any that score poorly.

In addition to traditional courses, Google acknowledges short attention spans and uses microlearning and whisper courses (trickle emails that reinforce learning points). They also vary the delivery medium to serve the audience and help employees build personal learning journeys.

All of this would potentially be a waste of time if Google did not then listen to its employees' ideas and actively test and validate new ideas at a high rate.

When Google or any other company combines a flexible approach to learning, personalization of content, and a true dedication to doing things in new ways that work, the results show up in the nimbleness and profitability of the company and the loyalty of the employees.

Implications For Intelligent Automation:

- What is different in your organization over what period?
- Do employees have learning journeys that extend beyond their specific roles?
- Do these include automation tools?
- Are changes rapidly evaluated and adopted, or do your teams crawl through broken glass to get approvals? Somewhere in between?

Baldrige Criteria: Focus On Success

Ensuring your organization's success now and in the future requires understanding the short and long-term factors that affect your organization and its marketplace. Success requires managing uncertainty and risk in the environment and balancing some stakeholders' short-term demands with the organization's and stakeholders' need to invest in long-term success.

Leaders Making This Real Today

Eric Kirsch is the chief investment officer of Aflac, a diversified insurance company. He and his team manage assets worth $120 billion. When Kirsch and I spoke, he shared an insurance industry maxim:

> *"Insurance companies don't go broke because they sell fewer policies from one year to the next. If they go broke, it is because their investments don't perform."*[68]

Focusing on results was never harder than when COVID became a recognized reality in early 2020, and the stock markets plummeted. On that day and for the weeks that followed, Kirsch had a huge problem on his hands. First, nobody on his team had ever lived through a global pandemic. Second, they looked to him to have the answers. This combination of events gave the role of risk management a whole new meaning.

Kirsch did what good leaders do—he communicated a sense of confidence mixed with humility and openness. While Kirsch had never been through a pandemic, he had been through several other conflagrations in his forty years on Wall Street. What he knew was most important was not to panic and to focus on the people and results.

The second important step he took was to open the floodgates of two-way communications between him and the team. In his words:

> *"I told them we were in this together and with your combined ideas, effort and commitment, we would make it through."*
> **Eric Kirsch, CIO, Aflac**[69]

Kirsch and team did make it through, partly because they did not panic and sell securities at rock-bottom prices and partly because they listened to each other. Kirsch kept the focus on achieving the results for the business while helping his team stay safe, calm, and confident that they could do it.

In another example, Brian Duperreault, chairman of AIG, a global finance and insurance company, shared a story of a business acquisition where the priority was to improve results.

In numbers reminiscent of the battle of Thermopylae, Duperreault's company of 600 people bought a company of 7,000 that was poorly run and greatly overstaffed. He knew that the only way to achieve acceptable results and keep this business running was a 35 percent reduction in people.

Duperreault's approach was direct, personal, and included face-to-face sessions with the acquired staff around the country. On trips from Houston to Chicago and Philadelphia, he spoke honestly and directly to the new employees about how the company he had just acquired had great potential to achieve its goals but not with the current staffing. He pointed out the process redundancy, "Checkers checking checkers," and overall lack of clear accountability. He even asked them, "You see what is going on here. What would you do?"

While the overall message was strong, the focus on results, the future, and his commitment to good business made the medicine go down better. In one memorable case, an executive from one of the units to be cut stood up and said, "I don't agree with you about my unit, but I like what you are saying, and I want to stay here and succeed."

While at times Duperreault thought he might be mobbed in those sessions, the result was worth it. When the cuts had been made and the new structure was in place, Duperreault said:

> *"It was like the clouds parted and light was shining on them.*
> *The bureaucrats and checkers were gone and they could do their jobs.*
> *When they came to work it was like a burden was lifted."*[70]

When all was said and done, the company did not miss a beat on results, and it is a great transformation story to this day.

Implications For Intelligent Automation:

- Does your organization understand the tradeoffs required to balance short and long-term success?
- Do they understand that automation is essential for long-term success and why?
- Are you candid?

Baldrige Criteria: Managing For Innovation

Innovation includes making meaningful changes to improve your products, services, programs, processes, operations, and business model to create new value for stakeholders. Innovation requires a supportive environment, a process for identifying strategic opportunities, and the pursuit of intelligent risks.

Leaders Making This Real Today

Taiyo Parts is a mid-sized Japanese manufacturer of industrial parts. The company was founded by Mr. Shirooka of Osaka in 1980. After years of steady profitability, the company struggled to innovate. Its employees were good at doing what many Japanese businesses do—avoiding risks and delivering high-quality products and services. Mr. Shirooka could see that what the company needed was more innovation, and innovation requires making mistakes. However, the Japanese culture frowns upon people making professional mistakes.

The founder's answer was to reward the "biggest mistakes" with a cash prize. For ten years, the company gave out an award for the biggest mistake of the last six months, which cost millions of yen. Nothing is lost in translation but more context will help.

The company is famous in Japan for its unusual work environment and is loved by millennials for breaking traditional and restrictive Japanese work practices. The point of the "Biggest Mistake" award was to lower the cultural resistance to taking chances, particularly if these chances could lead to better products and/or more profits.

The boundaries on the award are vague and only require that the mistake left behind knowledge for the company to use in the future, in this case, to not repeat. Therefore, the founder is not rewarding "stupid ideas" that have no connection to potential innovation. Instead, he rewards reasonably informed attempts to do new things.

In one example, an engineer lost the company millions over several years and won the prize four times. His colleagues rallied to his side to help him succeed, and eventually, one of his innovations made back multiples of the money he had lost. The result is a company that innovates at a higher rate than its competitors while attracting and retaining top talent.

In a similar example, Emily Lopez, director of leadership development at ConocoPhillips, told me that one big key to innovation in her company is "psychological safety." She defined this as people feeling comfortable to come forward to say what they think is important. The innovations she referred to include the whole range of good ideas that companies like ConocoPhillips need to thrive, and in many cases, prevent accidents. Lopez said:

> *"Psychological safety is a foundation and allows people to bring their whole selves to the job. This starts with listening to them to understand who they are and what they want and need. No psychological safety means fewer ideas, less feedback, dangerous physical situations, worst case scenarios."* [71]

Implications For Intelligent Automation

- Does your organization see how Intelligent Automation will help them provide better products and services to customers?
- Do your employees see themselves as part of the innovation or victims of it?
- Are your employers encouraged to suggest new ways of working or new products and services enabled by automation?

Baldrige Criteria: Management By Fact

Management by fact requires you to measure and analyze your organization's performance inside the organization and in your competitive environment. Analysis of performance measures and indicators should support organizational evaluation, alignment, and decision making.

Leaders Making This Real Today:

Managing by fact means more than the financial numbers. Kristin Johnson is the CHRO of Edward Jones, a financial services firm with 50,000 employees, including nearly 19,000 financial advisors. Her primary job is to make sure the company has the right people in the right roles and performing well. Johnson focuses on facts to avoid a climate where decisions appear capricious.

In the realm of HR, facts come in the form of financial performance, behavioral metrics, and client-facing metrics. While the numbers are easy to tally, the other categories can be more challenging. Johnson says:

> *"Historically some leaders have struggled to provide direct feedback supported by facts to help people grow as they should. Like any problem left too long, this can only get worse over time. We are focused on equipping our leaders to get better at providing direct feedback—it is a more human centered practice for sure."*[72]

She described a tough situation where a long-serving professional had not been given the feedback she needed to hear for years. When the time came and Johnson had to "bell the cat" by bringing the facts to the table, the situation was uncomfortable. This situation arises from inadequate feedback and too few facts over too much time.

Johnson provided another example of how Edward Jones continues to bolster its focus on performance and accountability. In a few rare cases, partners can ride on prior years' success and no longer contribute at the expected level. In these cases, facts are the neutralizing component of a potentially charged conversation.

Edward Jones has chosen to rely on a balanced combination of facts and subjective inputs to assess junior and senior staff. The results are a thriving business.

Laurent Freixe of Nestlé, mentioned above, provided another example where one of his company's units was no longer in Nestlé's strategic future.

The unit was in an eastern European country and the maker of a product steadily falling out of favor, specifically chocolate figurines like Santa Claus and the Easter bunny. Cute as these characters are, the market was ebbing away.

The factory happened to be a legacy of the Cold War era and provided primary employment for the town where it resided. The issue was sensitive.

For several months, Freixe met with the factory leaders to describe the situation and work toward a resolution, which was likely to be a sale or closure. Freixe described that the only way the conversations could be productive is if they were based on the facts of the situation. The factory leaders understood and became part of the effort to sell the company and retain the workforce. If Freixe had chosen to be opaque about the situation, the leaders would not have trusted him and not have provided their support.

In the end, the market for chocolate figurines began to improve, and with the collaborative focus on performance, supported by the facts, the factory was saved and is still producing products today. Ho, ho, ho, indeed.

Implications For Intelligent Automation:

- Are business decisions being made primarily based on facts or are they being made primarily based on emotion, ego, or whim?
- What do your best people honestly think?
- Are you seeking input from a variety of sources?

Baldrige Criteria: Societal Responsibility

Your organization's leaders should stress responsibilities to the public and the consideration of societal well-being and benefit. Your leaders should be role models for the well-being of your communities.

Leaders Making This Real Today

Raina Moskowitz of Etsy, Laurent Freixe of Nestlé, Roger Krone of Leidos, and Anita Lefebvre of Mercer Consulting are four leaders who told me how their company's success is measured by their numbers and growth and how they contribute to society.

For Raina Moskowitz, her four million sellers and millions of buyers make up the larger community and include a diverse rainbow of people—your and my neighbors—and it just so happens my daughter sells her products on the Etsy platform. Moskowitz and Etsy care about them all.

Laurent Freixe's responsibilities include business units in seventeen countries and many more individual communities. In each of these, he and Nestlé take an active interest, which again is reflected by his virtuous circle business award. One story he shared with me included Nestlé's active outreach in Columbia to try and deal with the controllable causes of violence in the region of Cali. Freixe does not do this simply because he abhors violence; he does this because that violence affects his employees and their customers.

Roger Krone works in a region and industry where people often cross from company to customer to neighbor over decades. He told me that while most often this means we simply think and act as members of the larger DC metroplex. How you treat people and what value your company demonstrates are part of that larger fabric.

While most of the time this leads to positive reinforcing behaviors, occasionally Leidos has had to separate people from the company for not living up to the company's values while living in the greater community.

Krone sees this as part of the company's responsibility, not to manage people's lives outside the office but to assure that Leidos and their people remain a beacon of integrity and higher values.

Anita Lefebvre described a recent demonstration of the commitment Mercer Consulting feels for its employees and the community. Specifically, the demand placed on the company during the COVID pandemic. The impact on the business was dramatic in the first few months and led to many plans to be reconsidered and business opportunities evaporating.

Some companies would have taken out the cost-cutting knife and created savings on the backs of their employees. Mercer's leadership took a different approach that Lefebvre described as identifying economic levers to pull in succession to adjust the numbers. Of these five levers, reducing headcount was the last one and only undertaken when every other lever could be thrown. Mercer was focused on the great good to the community and its employees and knew that in the end, this was best for the company and community.

As Lefebvre described, because the business saw all the measures taken to save the day, morale did not crater, and a sense of shared purpose was pervasive. When, at the end, some people did lose their positions, most people understood the necessity and respected the company for its empathetic handling of the situation.

Implications For Intelligent Automation:

- How will you prepare your people for the impact of automation, especially job loss?
- How will you treat people who no longer have a place in your company?
- Can you connect the benefits of Intelligent Automation to your larger community?

Baldrige Criteria: Ethics And Transparency

Your organization should stress ethical behavior by all workforce members in all stakeholder transactions and interactions. Senior leaders should be role models of ethical behavior, including transparency, characterized by candid and open communication on the part of leadership and management and by sharing accurate information.

Leaders Making This Real Today

The phenomenon of synchronicity occurs when like objects begin to resonate with each other for no obvious reason. A favorite example is what happens if you place two or more metronomes on a table, all moving differently. Over time, usually only a few minutes, the metronomes will all synchronize and be swinging from left to right and back. This phenomenon occurs not just in metronomes, fireflies, and starlings but also in the way people act.

Brian Duperreault, chairman of AIG, had several important points on ethics and transparency:

> *"People are tribal and they typically mimic what the leader does, this can become monkey see monkey do which is not necessarily bad unless the leader is."*

> *"If you blame others for your mistakes it will go through the company like wildfire. It is critically important to be true to who you are and what you say because people see right through you."*
> *"If what they see is real then that message percolates through the company, the same is true if they catch you being disingenuous."*[73]

Kimo Kippen, formerly of Marriott and Hilton, said:

> *"When self-awareness is there (in the leader) the magic starts to happen. Authentic leaders with integrity create followers and then the benefits cascade downward."*[74]

> *"People would walk through fire for a good leader. I know I did."*

Implications For Intelligent Automation:

- Do you have a 360 survey that is anonymous and confirms that ethical behavior is the norm?
- Do you exit people who violate this standard?

Baldrige Criteria: Delivering Value And Results

Performance results should be chosen and analyzed for you to deliver and balance value for your key stakeholders. Thus, results need to include financial measures and product and process results, customer and workforce satisfaction and engagement results, and leadership, strategy, and societal performance.

Leaders Making This Real Today

On this question, every leader I spoke to and every good leader I have worked for agree.

Whether it is oil and gas employees like those at ConocoPhillips; financial services employees at Assurant, Aflac, and AIG; hospitality workers at Marriott and Hilton; or management consultants, every good leader works every day to deliver value and results. It is easier to see those who don't—they go away in the short or long run.

The virtuous circle award given by Laurent Freixe at Nestlé is his approach, which in spirit is echoed by all the other executives I interviewed. What is your award?

Implications For Intelligent Automation:

- Do you have a balanced scorecard of results?
- Are your automation efforts showing benefits across your scorecard?
- Do you measure progress toward automation goals?
- Do you clearly act on shortcomings beyond financial metrics?

APPENDIX B
Acknowledgments

Books have authors, but authors have inspirations, coaches, and friends. I'm humbly honored to have worked with or come to know the people below and want to thank them for their support, inspiration, and examples.

- Chihiro Hodges
- William Conaty
- Henry DeVries
- Barak Eilam
- Julie Grzeda
- Gary Heffernan
- Jannik Henrik
- Phil Kilgore
- Charlotta Kvarnstrom
- Angela Leemans
- Commander Anne McKinney
- Kristian Mikkelsen
- Michael Murray
- Claudio Noriega
- Captain David Santucci
- Suzy and Jack Welch
- Colin Wooldridge
- Darren Wheeling

Special thanks to leaders I interviewed:
- Alan Colberg—CEO, Assurant
- Brian Duperreault—Chairman and former CEO, AIG
- Laurent Freixe—EVP and CEO Zone Americas, Nestlé
- Kristin Johnson—CHRO, Edward Jones
- Kimo Kippen—former VP HR Renaissance Hotels, Marriott
- Eric Kirsch—EVP and CIO, Aflac
- Emily (Knippel) Lopez—Director of Leadership Development, ConocoPhillips
- Roger Krone—CEO, Leidos

- Anita Lefebvre—CPO, Mercer Operations and Technology
- Raina Moskowitz—SVP, Etsy
- Bala Karthikeyan Nagarajan—HR Executive Director, General Electric
- Linda Passarelli—VP Talent Management, Fidelity Canada
- Penny Stoker— Global Leader of HR Services, EY

APPENDIX C
About The Author

Christopher Hodges is a C-suite consultant, corporate speaker, and business transformation expert. He is an authority on drawing out the best in people while successfully implementing technology and change. Christopher served as an officer in the US Navy, was an executive at General Electric, managing director at Accenture, and partner in Deloitte.

Applying lessons good and bad, from decades of international business, he helps leaders innovate their business, reduce risk, and maximize personal success.

Christopher's unique approach helps companies, executives, and teams transcend the technology of Intelligent Automation to achieve Noble Automation, a lasting, humanizing, and ultimately more profitable approach to technology adoption.

Beyond his inspired and practical talks, he helps companies navigate the uncertainty of technology change. Most importantly, he enables companies to achieve target ROI to remain competitive and retain and motivate top talent.

Christopher is also the author of *Placing Stones: Doing and Having What Matters Most* and the upcoming *One Sentence From Disaster: What Prevents Individuals From Living Their Potential At Work.*

He is a graduate of the US Naval Academy in Annapolis, Maryland, and the London Business School, United Kingdom.

Christopher has lived and worked in the United States, Japan, the United Kingdom, and Denmark. He now lives in Denver, Colorado, with his wife of thirty years, where they make every effort to appreciate the beauty of the Rocky Mountains and local microbreweries.

APPENDIX D
Executive Interviews

Colberg, Alan: CEO, Assurant; video interview with Christopher Hodges. 10-07-2020

Duperreault, Brian: Chairman and former CEO, AIG; video interview with Christopher Hodges. 9-24-2020

Freixe, Laurent: EVP and CEO, Zone Americas of Nestlé; video interview with Christopher Hodges. 10-02-2020

Johnson, Kristin: CHRO, Edward Jones; video interview with Christopher Hodges. 10-02-2020

Kippen, Kimo: former VP HR, Renaissance Hotels; video interview with Christopher Hodges. 9-22-2020

Kirsch, Eric: EVP, CIO Aflac; video interview with Christopher Hodges. 9-30-2020

Krone, Roger: CEO, Leidos; video interview with Christopher Hodges. 10-21-2020

Lefebvre, Anita: CPO, Mercer Operations and Technology; video interview with Christopher Hodges. 9-23-2020

Lopez (Knippel), Emily: Director of Leadership Development, ConocoPhillips; video interview with Christopher Hodges. 9-23-2020

McEvoy, Ashley: Executive Vice President, Worldwide Chairman, J&J Medical Devices; video interview with Christopher Hodges. 10-12-2020

Moskowitz, Raina: Chief Operations, Strategy and People Officer, Etsy; video interview with Christopher Hodges. 9-23-2020

Nagarajan, Bala: HR executive director, General Electric; video interview with Christopher Hodges. 9-25-2020

Passarelli, Linda: VP talent management, Fidelity Canada; video interview with Christopher Hodges. 10-05-2020

Stoker, Penny: global leader of HR Services; Talent Leader, Executive Functions, EY; video interview with Christopher Hodges. 10-05-2020

APPENDIX E
Works Referenced

1. McKinsey study on transformations https://www.mckinsey.com/business-functions/transformation/our-insights/perspectives-on-transformation

2. CEO Tenure https://www.pwc.com/gx/en/news-room/press-releases/2019/ceo-turnover-record-high.html

3. https://timeline.com/robots-have-been-about-to-take-all-the-jobs-for-more-than-200-years-5c9c08a2f41d

4. https://timeline.com/robots-have-been-about-to-take-all-the-jobs-for-more-than-200-years-5c9c08a2f41d

5. https://www.americanactionforum.org/insight/understanding-job-loss-predictions-from-artificial-intelligence/

6. https://www.usnews.com/news/economy/articles/2019-06-26/report-robots-will-replace-20-million-manufacturing-jobs-by-2030

7. https://www.usatoday.com/story/money/2017/11/29/automation-could-kill-73-million-u-s-jobs-2030/899878001/

8. https://www.c-span.org/video/?431119-6/elon-musk-addresses-nga&start=1493

9. https://www.americanactionforum.org/insight/understanding-job-loss-predictions-from-artificial-intelligence/

10. Freixe, Laurent. EVP and CEO Zone Americas of Nestlé, video interview with Christopher Hodges. 9-23-2020

11. https://www.businessinsider.com/what-self-serve-kiosks-at-mcdonalds-mean-for-cashiers-2017-6

12. https://www.cnbc.com/2017/06/20/mcdonalds-hits-all-time-high-as-wall-street-cheers-replacement-of-cashiers-with-kiosks.html

13. https://www.washingtonpost.com/business/2020/08/10/mcdonalds-ceo-lawsuit/

14. Max Tegmark, President of the Future of Life Institute, https://futureoflife.org/background/benefits-risks-of-artificial-intelligence/?cn-reloaded=1

15. Minto, Barbara. The Pyramid Principle: Logic in Writing and Thinking, 3rd edition

16. https://www.gallup.com/workplace/266822/engaged-employees-differently.aspx

17. https://blog.smarp.com/employee-engagement-8-statistics-you-need-to-know

18. https://blog.smarp.com/employee-engagement-8-statistics-you-need-to-know

19. https://blog.smarp.com/employee-engagement-8-statistics-you-need-to-know

20. https://blog.smarp.com/employee-engagement-8-statistics-you-need-to-know

21. Conaty, Bill, former CHRO General Electric, Personal Discussion with Christopher Hodges, used by permission.

22. https://www.surfertoday.com/surfing/why-do-waves-come-in-sets

23. https://www.nist.gov/system/files/documents/2017/02/09/2017-2018-baldrige-excellence-builder.pdf

24. Jack Welch, comment made to author in 1999.

25. Citizen Kane, Mercury productions, 1941.

26. Charlie Munger on Incentives https://quotefancy.com/quote/1561882/ Charlie-Munger-Show-me-the-incentive-and-I-will-show-you-the-outcome

27. Navy gun mount example: Naval Ordnance and Gunnery – NavPers 16116-B - US Government Printing Office, Washington 1952

28. Willie Sutton with Edward Linn, *Where the Money Was: The Memoirs of a Bank Robber* (New York: Broadway Books, 2004; first published in 1976 by Viking Press), page 160.

29. Philip Kilgore quote, used with permission.

30. Admiral Karl Donitz quote, https://www.goodreads.com/author/quotes/ 1727927.Karl_D_nitz

31. Tokugawa, Ieyasu example: https://tedium.co/2019/01/31/suggestion-box-history/

32. Krone, Roger, CEO, Leidos; video interview with Christopher Hodges. 10-21-2020

33. Freixe, Laurent, EVP and CEO Zone Americas of Nestlé, video interview with Christopher Hodges. 10-02-2020

34. "Tesla is still having trouble with robots," https://www.businessinsider. com/tesla-has-struggled-with-robots-breaking-down-at-car-factory-2020-3

35. "Remember the first robot disaster – GM plant in Fremont," https://www.upi.com/Archives/1982/03/03/Everyones-Out-at-GM-Fremont/7737383979600/, https://qz.com/1261214/how-exactly-tesla-shot-itself-in-the-foot-by-trying-to-hyper-automate-its-factory/

36. Susan Massie, *Trust but Verify: Ronald Regan and Me, A Personal Memoir* (Maine Authors Publishing, 2013). http://www.suzannemassie.com/books. html#

37. Sharon Mickan, "Evaluating The Effectiveness Of Healthcare Teams," June 2005, *Australian Health Review:* a publication of the Australian hospital association 29(2):211-7, https://www.researchgate.net/publication/7871878_Evaluating_the_effectiveness_of_health_care_teams.

38. Robert M. Pirsig, *Zen And The Art Of Motorcycle Maintenance* (William Morrow and Company, 1974). 0-688-00230-7

39. Colberg, Alan, CEO, Assurant, video interview with Christopher Hodges. 10-07-2020

40. https://www.gallup.com/workplace/266822/engaged-employees-differently.aspx

41. Jack and Suzie Welch, quote used by permission.

42. Gallup, https://www.gallup.com/workplace/284180/factors-driving-record-high-employee-engagement.aspx.

43. Gallup, https://www.gallup.com/workplace/284180/factors-driving-record-high-employee-engagement.aspx - amazing growth with several factors.

44. Black, Carol (2008) Working for a Healthier Tomorrow: Review of the Health of Britain's Working Age Population, http://www.workingforhealth.gov.uk/documents/working-for-a-healthier-tomorrow-tagged.pdf

45. Black, Carol (2008) Working for a Healthier Tomorrow: Review of the Health of Britain's Working Age Population, http://www.workingforhealth.gov.uk/documents/working-for-a-healthier-tomorrow-tagged.pdf

46. Kahn, William A (1990). "Psychological Conditions of Personal Engagement and Disengagement at Work" (PDF). *Academy of Management Journal.* 33 (4): 692–724. doi:10.2307/256287. JSTOR 256287.

47. Krone, Roger, CEO, Leidos, video interview with Christopher Hodges. 10-21-2020

48. Passarelli, Linda, VP talent management, Fidelity Canada, video interview with Christopher Hodges. 10-05-2020

49. Lefebvre, Anita, CHRO Growth Markets, Mercer, video interview with Christopher Hodges. 9-23-2020

50. Kirsch, Eric, EVP CIO, Aflac, video interview with Christopher Hodges. 9-30-2020

51. Gallup, 12 Questions for Employee Engagement, https://www.shrm.org/hr-today/news/hr-magazine/pages/0510fox3.aspx.

52. Kahn, William A (1990). "Psychological Conditions of Personal Engagement and Disengagement at Work" (PDF). Academy of Management Journal. 33 (4): 692–724. doi:10.2307/256287. JSTOR 256287.

53. Shine, Thomas Jr., USN retired; quote spoken to author and used by permission.

54. Campbell, Joseph *The Hero with a Thousand Faces*. (Princeton: Princeton University Press, 1949), p. 23.

55. Finding Joe, Director Patrick Takaya Solomon. Released September 30, 2011.

56. Duperreault, Brian, Chairman and former CEO, AIG, video interview with Christopher Hodges. 9-24-2020

57. Krone, Roger, CEO, Leidos, video interview with Christopher Hodges. 10-21-2020

58. Western Pennsylvania Conservancy https://waterlandlife.org/fallingwater/

59. Wright, Frank Lloyd. https://www.quotemaster.org/q08f79866b084c28cb5535a431d3ad4e0

60. Sinek, Simon. https://www.ted.com/talks/simon_sinek_how_great_leaders_inspire_action?language=en

61. "Hitler never gave the order, so who did?" WWII special Spartacus Olsson https://youtu.be/uQsGUndg_Vc

62. https://www.mckinsey.com/business-functions/mckinsey-digital/our-insights/intelligent-process-automation-the-engine-at-the-core-of-the-next-generation-operating-model#

63. Twain, Mark. https://www.goodreads.com/quotes/201777-i-ve-had-a-lot-of-worries-in-my-life-most

64. Hemingway, Ernest. http://www.cambridgeblog.org/2013/11/writing-tips-from-hemingway-fb/

65. Strategic Virtuous Circle Sculpture, Courtesy Laurent Freixe, Artist Glenda Léon, La Habana, and Madrid. http://www.glenda-leon.com/

66. Freixe, Laurent, EVP and CEO, Zone Americas of Nestlé, video interview with Christopher Hodges. 9-23-2020

67. Google Learning Culture https://edume.com/blog/google-learning-culture

68. Kirsch, Eric, EVP CIO, Aflac, video interview with Christopher Hodges. 9-30-2020

69. Kirsch, Eric, EVP CIO, Aflac, video interview with Christopher Hodges. 9-30-2020

70. Duperreault, Brian, chairman and former CEO, AIG, video interview with Christopher Hodges. 9-24-2020

71. Lopez (Knippel), Emily, Director of Leadership Development, ConocoPhillips, video interview with Christopher Hodges. 9-23-2020

72. Johnson, Kristin, CHRO, Edward Jones, video interview with Christopher Hodges. 10-02-2020

73. Duperreault, Brian, chairman and former CEO, AIG, video interview with Christopher Hodges. 9-24-2020

74. Kippen, Kimo, former VP HR, Renaissance Hotels, video interview with Christopher Hodges. 9-22-2020

APPENDIX F
Index